D0914863

"I've had the opportunity to work directly with Michael Alden on his children's book. His business know-how and ability to get things done is unparalleled."

—Naren Aryal, CEO Mascot Books

"As an entrepreneur and author myself, I would recommend *Blueprint to Business* to anyone who is in business or looking to start a company. Michael Alden's no nonsense approach is much needed for anyone who wants the real truth about the life of an entrepreneur."

—Ken Kupchik, author of *The Sales Survival Handbook Cold Calls, Commissions, and Caffeine Addiction—The Real Truth About Life in Sales*

"Michael Alden's story is truly inspirational. He has seen some extremely difficult times and has overcome extraordinary odds along his journey. He harnessed what he learned even as a young child to achieve great business success. The lessons in *Blueprint to Business* not only help those in business but it is for anyone who wants more out of life."

—June Archer, author of *YES! Every Day Can Be a Good Day: The Keys to Success That Lead to an Amazing Life*

"As a young entrepreneur, I have found that truly successful people help and teach others. Michael Alden has taken the time to help me with my business and my book. His experience is undeniable, and I would recommend *Blueprint to Business* to any entrepreneur who wants to learn from someone who has done great things and continues to."

—Casey Adams, Social Media Influencer and author of *Rise of the Young: How to Turn Your Negative Situation into a Positive Outcome, and Build a Successful Personal Brand*

"Being an entrepreneur has its challenges. Michael Alden shares his business experiences to help others succeed. His advice and enthusiasm is directed towards teaching and leading through example. If you are looking to succeed in business this book is a must read!"

—Christopher J. Wirth, entrepreneur, speaker, trainer, coach and host of the No Quit Living Podcast

"I've known Mike for over ten years. I have had the opportunity to work very closely with him on dozens of transactions. His ability to get things done and work through obstacles is second to none. When most people would give up, Mike figures out a way to get things done."

—Jim Shriner, television personality and author of *Live Disease Free Naturally*

BLUEPRINT
TO
BUSINESS

#BPTB

BLUEPRINT
TO
BUSINESS

AN ENTREPRENEUR'S GUIDE
TO TAKING ACTION,
COMMITTING TO THE GRIND,
AND DOING THE THINGS THAT
MOST PEOPLE WON'T

MICHAEL ALDEN

WILEY

Published by John Wiley & Sons, Inc., Hoboken, New Jersey
Published simultaneously in Canada

For general information about our other products and services, please contact our Customer Care Department within the United States at (800) 762-2974, outside the United States at (317) 572-3993 or fax (317) 572-4002.

Wiley publishes in a variety of print and electronic formats and by print-on-demand. Some material included with standard print versions of this book may not be included in e-books or in print-on-demand. If this book refers to media such as a CD or DVD that is not included in the version you purchased, you may download this material at http://booksupport.wiley.com. For more information about Wiley products, visit www.wiley.com.

Library of Congress Cataloging-in-Publication Data is Available:

ISBN 978-1-119-42492-5 (Hardback)
ISBN 978-1-119-42495-6 (ePDF)
ISBN 978-1-119-42498-7 (ePub)

Cover Design: Wiley
Cover Image: © belterz/iStockphoto

Printed in the United States of America

10 9 8 7 6 5 4 3 2 1

This book is dedicated to my amazing staff. Without my staff this book would not be possible. More specifically I would like to thank Shauna, Kayla, Garrett, Jeff, Jason, Chris, Linda, Asia, Steve and Korie. Your dedication and hard work is what made this book a reality. Thank you!

Contents

Introduction   xi

1   The Reality of Being an Entrepreneur   1

2   Getting Started   11

3   Business Basics   23

4   Action   37

5   To Know and Not to Do   53

6   What Is Success?   59

7   Opportunity   69

8   Failure   81

9   Do What You Say   91

10   Making Money Doing Nothing   111

11   Stop Caring   127

12   Lying to Our Children   141

More Resources   153

Index   157

Introduction

Growing up poor you would think I would have learned. Seeing my mom get eviction notices on our door in the projects you think I would have learned. Declaring bankruptcy in my late twenties you think I would have learned. Getting myself in millions of dollars in debt you think I would have learned. I've had more than a few Baba Booey moments in my life to say the least. But, there were many valuable lessons along the way. Like many things in my life I learned the hard way. This book is for those who want to learn from the mistakes of a real entrepreneur who started with nothing since the day I was born until now, generating millions of dollars.

It was mid-July 2016. I was about a month away from the launch of my second book. We had thousands of books presold and I was excited about the launch. I had just finished up a swim in my new pool in the house we had built. My girlfriend, Shauna, and I were getting ready to take the boat out for the day. It was hot, the sky was bright blue, not a cloud in sight, and the ocean was calm—just a perfect New England summer day. My businesses were rocking and things were great. Then I received a text from a vendor asking me when we were going to pay a small bill that was past due. He was one of the smaller vendors we dealt with, and he was looking for twelve thousand dollars owed. My companies have generated hundreds of millions of dollars, we have built brands, sold companies, and sold product all over the world. We had been in business since 2008 and done great things. When I received the text I thought that it must have been an oversight in our accounting department. I called accounting and found out it wasn't an oversight. We knew that we owed the money. Then I got a sick feeling in my stomach.

I was about to go out on the ocean all day and blissfully enjoy the fruits of my labor, when I realized that something was wrong.

In the very beginning, we had dealt with difficult financial obstacles that most businesses face when they do not have adequate capital. We bootstrapped things and struggled for years. But by 2016 things were great! Or so I thought. On that beautiful summer day in 2016, I realized that I had to dig in again and do the things that most would be unwilling to do. I obviously cancelled my boating excursion and went to the office. What I discovered made me even more physically ill. We were in much more debt than I had realized. Now, being in debt is not a big deal if you are aware of the debt and understand how to manage the debt, which I have done for years. But when a small vendor, a small-business guy with whom I have a close personal relationship, is stretched for twelve thousand, it's a problem. I tell you this story to give you the real-life experience of an entrepreneur. I want people to see what happens in business, and not just the great things. The great things come when you are able to work through the not so great things. As I write I have made some major changes in our business and business models. The great news is that these changes were not only necessary but also essential in order to survive in the current world. Some of the changes were very difficult to make. But with change comes opportunity, and with opportunity comes growth and stability. I have made many mistakes in my career and I want to highlight them so that you don't make the same ones.

CHAPTER 1

The Reality of Being an Entrepreneur

"We overcome, we adapt, we figure things out, we persevere. This is the life we choose."

—Michael Alden

One of my businesses that I learned the most from was Zeus Juice, the alcoholic freeze pop business. After years of research and planning, the product became a reality. I was finally making my freeze pops on Nantucket at a small distillery. I had a five million dollar machine that made the pops shipped to the island. It was quite a sight, taking up half of the warehouse space at the distillery. They were not happy about that. But after it was installed in early June, we began producing. I had already presold a bunch of product and I was pretty much out of cash. I had one of my brothers and my father there to help me with production. It was such a proud moment to see these alcoholic freeze pops flying off the production line and going into cases. After a couple hours, however, we had some challenges.

The most glaring challenge was that the product, which contained liquid, leaked. Well, some of them did. We had no option for sealing these packages ourselves, so we just ran as many pops as we could, and slowly, one by one, we inspected and cleaned them, then packed them into the cases. We were there for a week, and we stayed up the whole night on the last day to finish all the product we needed. At last, we loaded up the van to head back to the mainland. As soon as we got in the van, I knew we had a problem: there was a very strong smell of alcohol. Our quality control had failed to recognize microscopic leaks in the freeze pops and thousands of them were leaking. What was I to do? I was broke, had orders to generate cash, but had no cash to run more product. Well, what I did next is what entrepreneurs do: we figure it out.

DO IT AGAIN

When I arrived at my apartment, the cases had already started to collapse due to the leaking. I enlisted friends and relatives to help me inspect and clean the product again. We bought a couple of kiddie pools and filled them up with water and freeze pops. We tossed the bad ones and cleaned the good ones. But I knew I couldn't be sure if the leaker problem was solved. I decided to start freezing them. My initial plan had been to deliver the pops unfrozen so that consumers could take them home to freeze, but if they leaked that would never happen. So, for my first order I scraped up enough money to buy a small freezer, and I delivered the product already frozen with the freezer. The stores for the most part didn't care and kind of liked having a freezer in the store. Some stores even let me put product in their ice freezers. All that summer, that's what I did basically every day. I spent my early mornings cleaning, packing, and freezing, my days selling, and my nights promoting. By the end of the summer I knew it wasn't going to work anymore. We also had thousands of dollars of liquor and unfilled freeze pops sitting at the distillery, which wanted the machine out of their facility. They figured out that they could run the machine so that the pops came out all connected, like sausages, and they didn't leak. They ran the remaining product this way—long strips connected six wide by eight long—then boxed it up and sent it to a warehouse where I had rented space. I hadn't given up, but it was the end of the summer and I was still in law school and needed to finish, so I shelved the project.

ONE BIG ORDER

Another year had passed and I was in my final year of law school, but I had close to a hundred thousand alcoholic freeze pops sitting in a warehouse. In the previous year, I had sold them for a dollar each. During the fall, winter, and spring I searched for a distributor to pick up the product in Massachusetts. I was sending out samples when I had a few extra dollars to spare. Dozens of distributors said no, until one day one unexpectedly said yes. A distributor in Leominster, Massachusetts, called me back and set up a meeting with the owner, Jay. I figured out a way to get gas money, and came up with a plan to drive about an hour and a half to a place I honestly had never been before. Jay was a big guy wearing a velour jumpsuit, with a giant gold Star of David hanging from an equally large gold necklace. He welcomed me with open arms, and gave me a hug like I was his son. We sat down and discussed Zeus Juice. He asked how many flavors we had, and I said five but that we only had four in stock. He then asked me how many cases on a pallet. I had no idea. I instinctively said fifty. He said he would take four pallets. Now here was the challenge. I had no way to deliver the pops in their current form, and I had no retail packaging. When I was selling them the summer prior, they were literally in a plastic bag with a bar code sticker so that stores could ring them up. When I first started I hadn't thought through retail packaging, as I was only focused on bars and nightclubs. Jay told me he would pick up in two days. I almost threw up. I said I needed two weeks. Now, I was broke, I owed people money, and I had an order for $20,000. I was going to figure it out. That's what entrepreneurs do.

WHAT NEXT?

With no money, now in my last year of law school and a month before graduation, I had a chance to make a little money and pay off some debt. I had no car, no credit, no money, and barely enough food to live on. I was actually living on out-of-date Zone Bars. The Zone Diet Company was located in a building where I also had a part-time job. I had heard that they tossed their inventory that was out-of-date or slightly outside their weight requirements.

Every week I would go there to ask for their irregular bars, and they would gladly give me boxes of them. I ate them for breakfast, lunch, and dinner during this time.

With a large order that needed to be fulfilled, I reached out to friends, relatives, and neighbors. I borrowed a friend's car that not only had an expired inspection sticker and was unregistered, but the brakes were gone. A buddy who had been with me from the beginning of Zeus Juice asked his mom to give us gas money and some cold cuts to feed our helpers. The warehouse that was holding the Zeus Juice, to which I owed almost $3,000, allowed me to use their space so we could get the order ready. See, I owed them money, and they had my product. But it was worthless to them, and they were willing to help me so that they could get paid. In Chapter 9 I discuss debt and how to use it properly. I recruited my mom, my cousins, and my friends, who all agreed to help for nothing. Every day we went to the warehouse and hand-cut the freeze pops with scissors, then hand-sealed each and every one. When the day was done, we put them in baggies and let them sit overnight. The next morning, if there were leakers, we could find the source and localize the leak per baggie of ten, so that we wouldn't lose a whole case. It was a great morning when we didn't have leakers. It took us two weeks, ten to twelve hours a day, to get the order prepared. Finally, we were ready. I called Jay and scheduled the pick-up. We had four pallets ready to go. He sent his truck to pick up. His driver was getting ready to load the pallets when something unexpected happened. The warehouse refused to release the product without a check. A cashier's check. It was over—well, to some it was. I got ahold of the owner and promised him I would have the check to him by the end of the day. As collateral, I left him the only thing I had remaining: my friend's car! My buddy borrowed his mother's car. We drove to Jay's office to pick up the check for $20,000 and then couldn't get to the bank fast enough. Guess what? Another obstacle. The bank wouldn't just cash the check; it had to clear. I had promised the warehouse their check on that same day. I asked the bank to photocopy the check that we had deposited. I brought the copy to the warehouse and told the owner I would get him his check in a couple days. The deposit cleared, he got his check, some debt was paid, and I paid my buddy, I took about $500—and then a few months later I still had to declare bankruptcy. What's the point of this short story? I faced constant struggles, from being broke to not having transportation, to figuring out how to get there, to overcoming constant daily challenges. This is the daily life of an entrepreneur. As I type today, I have already put out fires with one of my businesses and it's only ten o'clock in the morning. This is the life. We overcome, we adapt, we figure things out, we persevere. This is the life we choose. It is rewarding, demanding, and sometimes devastating, but it's worth it.

WHAT ALLOWS ME TO SLEEP AT NIGHT

Despite business challenges and financial strains on some of my businesses, we have built a solid foundation. Building a long-term sustainable business that will survive for years, regardless of changes in the economy or business climate, is the "secret" to sanity for any entrepreneur. When you spend over $100 million to advertise products and services, as I have over the years, it should mean that whatever it is you are advertising has value to others. That is exactly what I have done over the years. I've built brands that add value to others. I'm advertising products and services that work and that people like and will continue to buy, so long as we are there to sell to them. Throughout this book I will discuss many of these products and the ups and downs. These real world stories will hopefully help you build your business and brand.

Stress—both personal and business—is what causes people to literally lose sleep. I have lost countless hours of sleep, suffered panic attacks and even bouts of depression, all due to the stress that comes with being an entrepreneur. It is an awesome responsibility when you have employees and people who count on you. But one thing that only you as the business owner can appreciate is the fact that ultimately you are responsible for everything and everyone. If things collapse, you will be the only one who really has to answer to your employees, your family, your friends, your partners, and your customers. No one else really has to answer. Because of the foundation I have built, this awesome responsibility that I have bestowed upon myself because of the life I've chosen is less daunting when I think about what it really means.

Tips in business that will allow you to sleep better:

1. Offer a great product or service that works.
2. Offer great customer service.
3. Improve when you can.
4. Look into the future.
5. Prepare for the future.
6. Respect the responsibility of being an entrepreneur.

WHO GETS PAID?

When building your business, you need to fully appreciate what I am saying. Understand that even though you are the only one who ultimately has to answer if things don't work, there are many other people involved. In *Rich Dad, Poor Dad*, Robert Kiyosaki tells people that they need to pay themselves first, and I respect that philosophy. But true entrepreneurs pay others first, especially those in your organization. True entrepreneurs sacrifice and barely make it in order to pay themselves later. Building a foundation over time allows you to sleep much better later, knowing that you have a solid business and product. One part of Kiyosaki's ideal that I fully appreciate is that at some point you must take care of yourself. Without you, the business would most likely never have started. You do have to ensure that you and your family will be protected. Sacrifice is a part of being an entrepreneur, but make sure when you are sacrificing that you are in fact building a foundation for the future.

If you're willing to make the sacrifice, this book is for you. Turn the page to take the leap and get started.

CHAPTER 2

Getting Started

IS AN IDEA A BUSINESS?

When you're thinking about business, what are some of the first things that you really need to think about doing? If you want to start a business, how do you start? What exactly do you do? A lot of people have a lot of great ideas, and they say, "I have this great idea and this is what I want to do." I had a guy come into my office one day and tell me that he had this amazing idea that he wanted to pitch to me. He set up an appointment to have me tell him what I thought about his business idea. He asked, "How many people sitting at their desk need to blow their nose? Or they need to wipe something?" I said, "A lot of people. That's what they have tissue dispensers for." He said, "No, no. What I want to create is a tissue dispenser that looks just like the bathroom toilet paper dispensers, like a roll, and I want to put it on the desk."

Now, I'm not one to rain on people's parades or be a dream stealer, but my first inclination, my gut feeling, was, "This is a ridiculous waste of time." He was excited about it, though, so I started asking him questions. When you start thinking about business, one of the questions that you have to ask yourself is whether there is a market for your product and service. In other words, do people need it? Do people want it? Will people buy a toilet roll dispenser for their desk?

When we think about innovators in business, we often think of Steve Jobs, who was an innovator and a visionary. People use the word "visionary" too freely, but Jobs truly was a visionary because he created things like the iPod, iPad, and iPhone. He created each because he felt that people needed and truly wanted it, but they just didn't know what *it* was. In other words, he created a market for the things he created. MP3 players were out before the iPod, but what Steve Jobs created with iTunes and that business model was something that people didn't really understand that they wanted until they tried it. That's rare. It can be done, but it's very rare.

When you're thinking about a business or a service, you have to ask, "Is there a market for this business?" When I first started out in business, as discussed in Chapter 1, one of the products that I had was a freeze pop with alcohol in it, called Zeus Juice. It's a frozen shot, 8.2 percent alcohol, frozen solid. When I showed it to anyone, the first thing they did was to tell me their opinion about chemistry. They said, "Alcohol doesn't freeze." Well, this freezes solid even though it's 8.2 percent alcohol, and it tastes amazing, just like a freeze pop. When I first started this business I tried to find others actually doing this in the marketplace. I couldn't find anybody in the United States making them. I'm no Steve Jobs and a freeze pop with booze is no iPod or iPhone, but no one else was doing it and people loved the product.

When I was building that business, I sat down with a friend who's a very successful businessman in multiple businesses from real estate, to seafood, to casinos. He said to me, "Mike, is anyone else doing it out there? If people aren't doing it there is usually a reason why. Why hasn't anyone done it?" Well, I searched and searched. I found a company in the Netherlands that was doing really well in Europe with the exact same thing. That was a great sign. They were selling a freeze pop with booze in it, which they called Freaky Ice. I decided to look at their model to see how they were doing it and what sort of mistakes, if any, they had made.

I've had a lot of people tell me a lot of things in my career, but one of the most profound things that I've learned is that success in business and in life can be duplicated. Success can be duplicated. I looked at the Freaky Ice product. I went to their website, called their company and "infiltrated" it, and I asked a lot of questions. I looked at what they had done and saw some of the mistakes they had made, and I tried not to make those myself when I moved forward with the business.

Business Building Tip

Success can be duplicated.

Business Building Tip

People like to talk about their business. Get them talking!

I also examined other businesses in the same category of novelty alcoholic products. Even though I was somewhat stealthy in trying to see what these outfits were doing, I located several different businesses and I called them. Now this all started in the late nineties when businesses Internet presence isn't what it is today. You couldn't find all the information that you can find now. The thing I learned —and it has paid dividends over and over again—is that entrepreneurs and business people like to talk about their business. If you can build a rapport with someone and ask for help, most will say yes. A gentleman in Florida named Ray was selling a shot in a test tube and was very successful. I was essentially hoping to compete with him. He didn't see it that way. He mentored me for hours and hours over the phone, educating me on the ins and outs of the liquor industry. Why? Business people, especially successful ones, love to tell others how they did it and even help young entrepreneurs. It's not always their ego, either; often it's because they too were green and needed help, and someone taught them, so they are paying it forward. When thinking about your business, ask others, even strangers, in the same or similar business for help, and odds are they will help.

DON'T JUMP COMPLETELY IN

A lot of people who have that entrepreneurial spirit and a great idea want to really run with it. When I started Zeus Juice, I was in law school, I had a job, and I slowly began to build the business. Weekends and nights, I started to go through the whole process, learn about the business, get my website built, and get my packaging design. Now, the alcohol business is not like selling pens and pencils; there's a whole regulatory nightmare that you have to go through. I learned the whole process with the help of others while still in law school and maintaining my real job and current income. I made a ton of mistakes, from filling out the paperwork incorrectly to inadvertently not disclosing relevant information, to having my formulas rejected due to submitting ingredients that were not on the approved list. But I learned it, slowly. I've mentored many young entrepreneurs and have told them that you can work your main income stream to the best of your ability AND start to build the business you are passionate about.

YOU CAN BE PART-TIME AND PASSIONATE

I spoke at an event where people paid up to $10,000 per seat to attend. During the question-and-answer session, an aspiring musician asked if he should just give up everything and only focus on music. I asked: Do you have bills? Do you need money to eat? Can you pay your bills with music now? He had bills, and music wasn't paying those bills. My advice, much to the chagrin of some of my fellow panelists, was to keep doing what was paying the bills and work the music nights and weekends. I told him he could be passionate about his music and push hard with his passion, but to keep money coming in to sustain his lifestyle. You can do both: you can work part time on your idea, your passion, while maintaining your day job and lifestyle.

There are a lot of people who get really excited, who are very emotional about their ideas, and they want to go ahead and just jump right into it. They're going to make a full-on effort, but the biggest challenge that most young entrepreneurs face—and it's the exact same challenge that I also faced with Zeus Juice—is lack of capital. When I first started Zeus Juice in the early 2000s, I told myself I only needed $90,000 to launch the business. I did the math over and over and over again. I will say this, folks: math is not my strong point. The same friend who asked me, "Mike, are there other people out there doing it?" also said, "Whatever you think you need for your business, multiply it by three, and maybe four, and then you might be able to get it started." If you think you need $100,000, you probably need $300,000 or even $400,000. That's scary. Most people don't have that kind of money. But that is the reality. Undercapitalization is one of the biggest reasons why most businesses don't succeed.

When I started Zeus Juice, I didn't know anybody, I didn't have any big-time investors, and I didn't have the ability to access capital—I didn't have any of that stuff. I also wasn't going to allow this lack of capital to kill my vision for this business. Don't let money or capital be your barrier. Don't let money stop you from pursuing your goals. Let me repeat, don't let money prevent you from moving forward, but be cognizant of the fact that you do need money in this world in order to be successful. This is essential, but often overlooked.

ELF ON A SHELF

I have a friend who came up with an ingenious idea similar to that of the smash hit Elf on a Shelf. It targets a different holiday altogether and is not religious specific. He created a doll that would be used similarly to that of the Elf on the Shelf. He had a story line created. It's fun, and I certainly think it has legs. He pitched it to me and I 100% believe that it has legs and could be huge. Many times businesses are created on the backs of other businesses and success can be duplicated. Following the Elf on a Shelf model but with what I believe is a much broader audience could be huge for my friend. I recently asked him where he was at, and he said if he just had the money to launch it he would consider it. Now, you might be saying, why don't I invest in it? Great question. I own multiple businesses, including CloiXonné which is exploding as I type, so I need to focus my time and efforts on what is working for me. Plus, I've invested in friends and family business ventures before and if things go wrong, they really go wrong. But, with this deal in particular, my friend could easily raise the money he needs to get started and he can do it part time. Do not let money slow you down or prevent you from achieving your goals!

WAKE UP

I'm tired of people telling you to dream big. A dream is just a dream. It isn't reality. Chasing after a dream is the wrong way to think about whatever it is you are trying to accomplish. When I was a kid I used to dream about winning the lottery and what I would do with the money. I used to dream about being rich. I was going to buy a big house for my mom, and then a house for my dad. I was going to buy a plane so I could fly anywhere. These are all dreams from a kid growing up poor. Successful people don't dream, they do. Stop dreaming big; start thinking and DOING big things. When you wake up from your dream and realize that we live in the real world, then things start to happen.

GREAT IDEA, BUT...

I had a friend, a business associate who launched a website selling shoes. It was a great website offering all different types of shoes. My friend spent thousands and thousands of dollars on developers, and on working out deals with different shoe companies, wholesalers, and all these great things. He had a half-decent name for it, too.

Now how do you get people there? Just because you have a cool website and even a cool product doesn't mean anything. You get people there by spending money, spending marketing dollars to attract potential customers. That's how you do it. That's where the money comes into play: you need capital to launch a business, but don't let it stop you. If you can't come up with the money right away, it doesn't mean you can't do marketing, but you just need to be aware of it. People would argue and say marketing can now be done with social media. That is true, but just like reality television, social media isn't really what it seems. The businesses out there that are making a play on social media, the ones making money selling products on social media, are paying for all if not most of their posts, tweets, snaps, and check-ins. Don't be fooled into thinking that you can just create a "buzz" on social media because you have a cool product or service. There are thousands of cool products and services that we will never hear about, simply because they lacked the funds to create a real marketing campaign. Gary Vaynerchuk, the leading social media expert, acknowledges that even he spends money to promote his brand and has been working at it for years, at a pace that most people wouldn't be able to keep up with or even want to try. In Chapter 10 I give you what I believe is the best advice as it relates to marketing anything.

DON'T QUIT YOUR DAY JOB

If you're an entrepreneur in your twenties or thirties and you have a job, do not leave your job until your business is generating enough revenue to pay your bills. I use this age group because time and time again, I see young people in the workforce decide to follow a dream and quit their day jobs, thinking they are going to be an overnight success. Business is really hard. Words cannot effectively communicate how hard it is, but when you take away your income, the situation gets almost impossible. Leaving your job before your business is generating enough revenue to pay your bills is ludicrous and asinine. It's not dedication. People say, "I'm really dedicated. I'm dedicated to my business so I want to go straight into it." It's a silly and potentially dangerous idea; don't do it. I saw this guy with a decent job making $50,000 a year. He had a business idea and quit his job before he even had his business set up. Then he came to me and said, "Mike, I'd like you to show me how to start and move forward with the business." I said, "But you left your job. Why'd you do that? Why'd you leave your job? I don't understand." He said, "Well, you know, I really wanted to do this full time." I said, "Yeah, but you have no business prospects. You don't even have the equipment you need to actually sell the product that you wanted to sell."

Again, there's something to be said for the entrepreneurial spirit. It's a great thing. A lot of people don't have that type of spirit. If you do, *don't* be stupid. People are going to make mistakes; I do so every single day. But don't make the mistake of quitting your job until your business is ready. Let's go back to my Zeus Juice idea. I had a full-time job making about the same amount of money as the guy I just mentioned, about $50,000 a year. I was going to law school at night. I set up the business, and one of the things I did was to make sure that I had revenue coming in before I left my job.

My mistake was I didn't have *enough* revenue or enough capital. I was young, naive, and driven, but I was going to do it and I didn't want to be one of "those guys" that said, "If had only done that." This is something that you really need to think about. When you're looking at the big picture and you look at your idea, you don't want to be that guy thirty years from now, sitting on your front porch and saying to yourself, "I had a great idea and I should've done it." To me, that is one of the scariest things I can think about. Marshall Goldsmith a *New York Times* best-selling author and one of the top executive coaches in the world said something very profound to me on my podcast The Alden Report. He said: "In life old people don't regret the risks they took and failed, they regret the risks they failed to take." This book isn't designed to kill your idea or your vision. Rather, it's designed to give you real advice from a real entrepreneur. Use my mistakes and my experiences to your advantage. This is real life stuff, from a real guy. I didn't just jump into starting Blue Vase Marketing; it was years in the making and throughout this book you will learn how.

Over the last few pages, you've said to yourself:

- Is there a market for my business?
- Is anyone else out there doing it?
- Can I learn from them?
- Do I have enough money to do this?
- Is it a viable business?
- Is it something that I'm really willing to do?

Write that last question down and think long and hard about it. Are you willing to take risks, sacrifice relationships, and commit?

In the next chapter, I'll lay out the fundamentals of setting up a business. We're going to talk about intellectual property, trademarks, copyrights, and patents. These are things that too many people don't think about and when they do, it may be too late.

CHAPTER 3

Business Basics

The fundamentals of business aren't that complicated. Setting up a business isn't that complicated. Protecting your business isn't that complicated. Filing the proper paperwork with the state and federal government isn't that complicated. This section of the book will highlight the things you need to think about when starting out or even if you are already in business now.

PROTECTING YOUR BUSINESS

When you're building a business, a legitimate business, you have to ask, "What do I need to do in order to protect myself"? I'm a lawyer, but this isn't going to be legal advice. If you do have concerns or aren't sure about the process, you should consult with a local attorney. That said, you can do a lot of what's necessary on your own; lawyers make you think that you need a lawyer for everything, but much of it is not that complicated. I did a lot of these things before I was even a lawyer myself. All that being said, if you are ready to start a business, it would be worth a few hundred dollars just to sit down with a business lawyer.

Business Building Tip

Lawyers aren't necessary for business, but consulting with one in the beginning is worth every dollar spent.

Let's say you have an idea. The first thing you need to do is to set up a company. Being a sole proprietor—in other words, running a business as an individual person with no official status—is one of the craziest things you can do. I don't care if you're a landscaper, a plumber, or a hairstylist renting a chair at the local barbershop. I don't care what it is, but operating a business as a sole proprietor is absolutely ridiculous. It puts you in harm's way, and it puts your family in harm's way. Setting up a business entity is simple, and it can be effective at protecting you and your family from potential lawsuits in the future. It's also a great way to help grow your business.

NAMING YOUR BUSINESS

One of the very common areas where entrepreneurs make big mistakes is in coming up with the name of their business. Often someone has already come up with the same exact name that you came up with, believe it or not. And they are using it. Whether it is a domestic company that incorporated in one of the fifty states or even an international company doing business here, an existing business could already have the name. If you are in this early stage of naming your business, I would recommend engaging an attorney to help you with the search of your business name. You may have limited funds now, but just imagine being a growing business and all of a sudden finding out there is another business with the exact same name. It happens all the time and can be avoided.

We'll talk more in a little bit about your company name later in this chapter when we get to aspects of trademark, branding, and intellectual property.

Once you've chosen a name, protect yourself by creating a separate official entity: incorporate or start a limited liability company (an LLC). I'm a big fan of limited liability companies.

I'm a fan not just for the reason that a lot of people assume, because it "limits your liability"; you could do that with an S corp or a C corp. I like the limited liability company for a couple different reasons. One of the biggest ones is that if you start an LLC and you're a single member, you can essentially operate your business *as if* you were a sole proprietor. In an S corp or a C corp, there are certain "corporate formalities," resolutions, and by-laws, and other things that are so archaic or difficult for a single member that they're not worth your time.

We're not going to really get into the nitty-gritty legal stuff like your operating agreement and the complexities there, but if I were you, I would set up an LLC in Delaware. Some people like Nevada, because of the anonymity factor. But in a lot of states, a Nevada business still has to file as a foreign entity anyway; in any state in the union, you can still operate with a Delaware LLC. Filing in Delaware is easy, and it's cheaper than in most states. It's also where the LLC was established, so there's a lot of case law out of Delaware related to the topic. You can form your LLC yourself on Delaware's website.

Once you've officially established your LLC, you'll receive Articles of Organization (for an LLC). It sounds complicated, but its usually just a one page document.

Once you've formed your LLC, what next? Next you need to secure an EIN (Employer Identification Number) from the Internal Revenue Service (IRS). This is something, again, that you can do yourself. You go right to the IRS website, you file some paperwork, and you show them your formation documents and they will issue you an EIN.

You have your company name, your formation documents, and your EIN; now you need to go to the bank and open an account. Most banks will tell you exactly what you need to open the account. Generally it's the EIN and proof of formation. Some will ask for the actual by-laws or articles of organization. Now you have a business bank account. When you start making money, people write checks to the name of the business, not to you.

Once you've set up the business, keep in mind that there are great tax benefits to having a business. Benefits include write-offs, tax incentives, and tax breaks depending on the type of business you are in. Look into your business and see if incentives are available. Some states offer tax breaks to new companies, and some municipalities will do the same. Spend a little time and do the research.

INTELLECTUAL PROPERTY

A lot of people overlook, or don't understand, the intellectual property side of their business, and it drives me insane. This is in many respects the most important part of your business. Coca-Cola's most valuable assets are its trademark and its formula. The formula is almost impossible to truly protect, especially in this day and age, though they've certainly done a very good job at that. I would argue that the most valuable asset of Coca-Cola (now I'm talking about the brand, not Coca-Cola the company, because they own many other things) is their trademark.

As you close your eyes, you can envision that "Coca-Cola" logo; it's in cursive, it's beautiful. It's been around for more than a hundred years. It's probably one of the most recognizable trademarks in the world next to, what? Anybody know? McDonald's Golden Arches. Those are two extremely valuable things, the Golden Arches and the Coca-Cola trademark.

When you come up with a product and business name, trademarks can be the most valuable asset of your entire business. Apple Inc. had a big trademark dispute overseas with another company that was also called Apple, and they ultimately settled for millions of dollars, because the other company had actually started before them. Your trademark is something that you really, really need to think about.

Think about what the name is going to be of the product or the service, or even the company. Spend some time researching whether any other product is out there with that name.

There are laws and statutes and a ton of case law that deals with trademarks. You see, when you become an attorney, you don't know everything. I certainly don't know everything. I'm not giving you legal advice; this is more on the business side of things, with a little legal twist to it. Trademark law is very, very important. It needs to be thought about from the very beginning.

IT'S THE BORING STUFF THAT MATTERS

I had an aspiring young entrepreneur reach out to me and ask for my help with the basics of business. He wanted help with the really boring stuff like setting up bank accounts and forming an LLC. I agreed to help because he was a friend of a friend. When he came to my office it was clear he was dreaming about what he thought his life would be like. He wouldn't listen to most of my suggestions, but I pleaded with him to ensure he had his intellectual property buttoned up. He assured me that he had a great name and logo for his company. He said his girlfriend had it all covered. She graduated from college, which somehow made her an expert on intellectual property. Now, the business he was starting was essentially a marketing company, and his brand and logo were a crucial part of his entire business model. After my meeting he left and "started" his business. About a year passed and he came to me frantically with a cease and desist letter from a pretty big law firm demanding that he not only stop using his name but also his logo. If the suit were successful, the other company would effectively put him out of business. The good and bad news is that this guy, although he formed a business, didn't really have a business, and so he didn't have much to worry about. But if he had just taken the time and spent a little money on his intellectual property, he would not have had to be concerned.

Robert Kiyosaki lists in his book *Rich Dad Poor Dad* (Chapter 3, pp. 121 © 9/18/2015. This cite was from the digital version.) assets one should acquire to build wealth. One of those assets is intellectual property. With intellectual property you can get paid residual income and royalties for years. Every time a song plays on the radio, or a television program airs, or a book is sold, the owner or creator is paid a royalty from the entity that used the intellectual property. What other intellectual property do you have? The thing that makes most entertainment people rich, really rich, is copyrights. The word itself explains what it is: the rights that people retain for their copy, and that pertains to music, television, books, movies, and more. It pertains even to software in many instances. If you create content like the book I'm creating right now, you need to copyright it. Again, there is case law, statutory law that deals with both copyright and trademark, and not filing for either one is a huge mistake. You actually have copyright as soon as the content is created and distributed, but you cannot get damages in a potential lawsuit unless you have it registered.

There are companies out there that buy patents from other companies, and then they go out and sue other companies for patent infringement. These are publicly traded billion-dollar companies. People call them patent trollers. They're worse than ambulance chasers, but this is what they do. They make billions of dollars because people didn't spend the time on the front end, in the very beginning, to actually think about whether or not they have a trademark right, or a copyright, or a potential patent that they could file.

PATENTS

Do you have something that is patentable? Do you have a widget, a gadget, something that has some sort of utility? Business patents are out there. They've been eroded recently; through recent case law, it's been said, "You can't patent a business model." Patents are for movable things. We're talking about computers. We're talking about things that have utility, widgets or gadgets, whatever it is. Patent law is more complicated than copyright and trademarks. If you do have something that is in the idea stage and you think it has utility, consider at least a patent search to see if there is anything similar out there.

Trade secrets (the formula of Coca-Cola), and trade dress (the design of the Coca-Cola can) aren't patentable. There are a lot of different variables that entrepreneurs don't think about. When it's too late, when potential lawsuits happen, things can get really, really ugly, and it can cost you millions of dollars. It can cost you your business. Now again, to be clear, patent law was not anything I practiced regularly, and by the time this goes to print things may even change. But, the purpose of this is to make you aware and understand the importance of your intellectual property.

A BOTTLE IS JUST A BOTTLE, RIGHT?

An old business associate in the alcohol business made a rookie mistake that caused him to have to change his whole product line. He created an awesome product, and his trade dress is very similar to the trade dress of another product. That company noticed his trade dress, which was his bottle, and sent him a cease and desist letter. His bottle was just a rectangular bottle. It was very distinctive looking, with thick glass and a matching silver cap. That bottle really jumped off the shelf. He had made tens of thousands of bottles that actually infringed on a patent that another company held. Who would have thought you could patent a bottle? Well, the company that designed the bottle thought enough of its distinctive design to patent it.

To make matters worse, his trademark also infringed on another company's trademark. He had the trademark embossed into the glass of the bottle. This meant that even if he could work out a deal with the company that had the patent issue, he still had an issue with the company that held the trademark. If he had known about these intellectual property concerns, if he had talked to an attorney before, or if he had spent some time researching, he probably wouldn't even have this issue. He will have to modify the way his product looks as a result of a possible infringement. He got off kind of easy, as it is early on in his brand development. But, if he had decided to go big, and grow the business fast, he could have had major problems. The penalty for patent and trademark infringement is all of the revenue. Not just a fine—ALL OF THE REVENUE! He also had several investors who had put a significant amount of money into this product line, and he had to explain to them his rookie mistake. Moral of the story: research, research, research. It isn't sexy, but it's necessary to spend time on the research.

WE'RE JUST MAKING MUSIC

I have a friend who's a successful musician. He came to me and wanted me to invest in a new album. I asked him, "Well, who owns your copyrights?" He said, "I don't know." I said, "What about the trademarks? You've got some really cool trademarks." He didn't know. I said, "How do you not know that? How do you not know who owns your copyright? I'll tell you right away who most likely owns it—the distributor. Maybe the record producer actually owns the copyright, but the trademark—who owns that? Who owns your name?"

My musician friend is very successful rapper Esoteric, and his brand is Czarface™. Esoteric feeds his family with his music and his brand, so protecting them is crucial. After we talked he got to work figuring out his intellectual property world. His brand and branding are very interesting. He has created a personal brand with his rapping and music as Esoteric and a larger brand, which encompasses his DJ, 7L, and other successful rappers including Inspectah Deck from the Wu-Tang Clan under the umbrella of Czarface. The design of his albums is brilliant. It's not just music; Czarface is a comic book character and the albums have the look and feel of a comic book.

Following the Robert Kiyosaki method of creating content and investing in intellectual property in many different ways, they got the attention of Marvel Comics. So much so that, as a result of their brand and their music, they now have a song featured in the movie *Black Panther*. Without creating intellectual property that was properly protected, this deal most likely would not have happened. By the time this book is published the movie will have been released and Esoteric, 7L, and Czarface will most likely be household names. When I asked Esoteric how the Marvel deal happened, he said: "Marvel has been tuned into hip-hop for a while, and they work closely with Method Man, who recommended Czarface.... They have been releasing a series of homage/tribute covers to legendary groups like NWA, Public Enemy, Wu-Tang Clan, and more, and Czarface was lucky enough to be featured as a cover and in a another issue." I don't consider what happened luck—it was the creation of intellectual property.

WHAT ABOUT YOUR NAME?

You can get on the United States Patent and Trademark Office website and look at Michael Alden and see that I actually own my name. Successful people, especially those who are in the public domain or plan on being in the public domain, trademark their own names. The WWE, which used to be the WWF, lost a huge trademark dispute to the World Wildlife Fund and it cost millions to dispute and defend. The somewhat ironic part of this is that the now WWE's entire business model is based on creating intellectual property and protecting it. This includes owning the actual names of some of the wrestlers, like John Cena. That's his given birth name and they own it! Notice when Dwayne Johnson is in the movies he no longer uses Dwayne "The Rock" Johnson? That's because the WWE owns "The Rock" and use of it would mean there would have to be royalties paid.

WHAT ABOUT MY WEBSITE?

When thinking about your business or product name, a website is critical. Several years ago I had clients who had a product they were excited about. They had created a television advertisement, had the product designed and formulated, created brochures, and mapped out the marketing strategy. Upon my advice they also applied for the trademark. One thing they forgot was to register the domain name. When they went to register the domain they noticed that another marketer had taken the name. Without getting into the legal aspect of what they could have done, they had a problem. There are laws that speak to this very issue and protect brand owners. But they didn't have the time for a legal battle. After many discussions with the owner of the domain, I brokered a deal to buy it from him. This cost my clients a lot of money and heartache. They could have registered the website months prior, but just let it slip. Whatever your business or product idea, register the domain prior to rolling it out.

Business Building Tip

Register several iterations of your website, including misspellings, and things like www.buymyproduct.com or www.trymyproduct.com. Spending a few dollars now even if you don't move forward can save you from future problems and make you millions later.

AN IDEA—WHAT DOES IT MEAN?

If you have a great idea and you feel like you're ready to do it—you're willing to make the sacrifices, put your family on the line, put your house up, do all these things—then you have that entrepreneurial spirit. The blood is pumping through your veins. You are that guy, or you are that gal, and you are ready to take that step. You're going to form the business. You're going to go out there and you're going to make it. You're going to do something. Don't go out there and do it without at least having the proper, basic fundamental setup that we've discussed throughout this chapter.

ARE YOU SURE YOU WANT THIS?

Having taken all the official steps, now you're a legitimate business. I had one guy who came to me for advice who wanted to get into the marijuana business. I spent countless hours counseling him about this. Now, I'm not one to advocate for substance usage, but the marijuana business is obviously the next gold rush, so it's an interesting industry to get involved in. The potential profitability is huge. In fact CloiXonné recently launched its own full spectrum hemp based canabidiol (CBD) spray, and it is making a lot of people a lot of money who are ambassadors with my company. There are obviously a lot of medicinal benefits from the cannabis plant. Even though I knew nothing about that world, I saw the opportunity, researched it, found people who knew more than me and launched an amazing product within the CloiXonné product line that is also helping a lot of people while making a lot of people money.

After several hours talking with this guy I realized that he was just a pothead; he had silly ideas, no business acumen, and no business being in business. Entrepreneurship isn't a fantasy or a dream, it's a real thing. You don't have to be brilliant, but you must have focus, vision, and drive. We're talking about how to set up a business. We're talking about some of the basics of starting a business, some of the things to think about. Being an entrepreneur, being your own boss, being responsible for generating revenue, being responsible for the people that work for you, their families, and their children: these all add up to a big responsibility. A lot of people can't handle it.

There's nothing wrong with that. Being an entrepreneur is a different type of mentality. It's a different type of stress. Simply reaching the point where you have a business does not make you an entrepreneur. But you're on your way. You've done more than what most people have. You've protected yourself. You're starting. We'll talk a little bit more about the mentality of an entrepreneur and what it really takes to become a successful entrepreneur in the next chapter.

CHAPTER 4

Action

One of the biggest challenges in life and in business is that people lack the ability to take action, to actually do something. You see, a lot of people think about wanting to be successful, and they talk about it. They dream about accomplishing their goals but they never actually do anything. The trick is, you actually have to do something in order to accomplish your goals. It sounds so simple, doesn't it?

One of the most basic things that a lot of people think about is maybe losing weight. The only way you're going to lose weight is if you actually do something. You're not just going to lose weight by doing nothing or by doing the same thing over and over again. It doesn't happen that way. Our bodies are designed to be worked so that we are able to do things with our body. When you want to lose weight, you need to do a little bit more than what you were doing previously. You need to eat less. You need to take action and actually do something. I have found, again and again, in life and in business, that this is one of the biggest barriers that most people are having a tough time overcoming: taking action.

DUMPSTER DIVING

One of my favorite jobs as a kid was working at Chuck E. Cheese's. It is truly amazing the things I learned there, from the importance of a system, to being punctual, to recognizing an opportunity. One hot summer day my manager called an impromptu meeting with the kitchen staff. It was a weekday during the summer so we weren't that busy. He discovered that over the weekend we had apparently tossed out the old food and trash into the wrong dumpster, and the trash company would not pick up the dumpster. He didn't explain why, but he said all of the trash in the dumpster had to be removed from one dumpster and put into the empty one. There were only a few of us working, and we all looked at each other to see who would step up. I would be lying if I said I immediately stepped up. But after some cajoling from my manager, I agreed to literally go inside a dumpster that was filled to the top on a hot summer day and empty it out by hand. To this day I know that smell of rancid food and trash. I made a makeshift hazmat suit with trash bags and dove in. I was removing trash for a couple of hours. People on staff came out to see if I really was in fact doing it and laughed at me. If there were camera phones back then I'm sure there would have been a bunch of pictures taken and posted on social media. Why did I do it? Why would I do it? It was a day that wasn't busy, and I knew the manager was possibly going to send some of us home. But I needed and wanted the money. At fifteen or sixteen years of age I wasn't thinking about the moral of this story or what I was teaching myself or others. Plain and simple, I wanted to work and make money. I did what others wouldn't so I could make a little extra money. That little extra money and willingness to do what others wouldn't, in addition to my work ethic in general, earned me a lot more than just a few hours that day. I took action, even if it was gross, unglamorous, and embarrassing. And as a result, I was given more opportunities for extra hours, including tasks that others wouldn't do.

What do I mean by action? It has two categories: there's the mental side of action, which has to come first, and then the physical side of action. For instance, top professional chess players typically visualize and go step-by-step in a hypothetical chess game, in order to see what could possibly happen. They mentally prepare themselves for the physical action that will eventually take place. It's a critical part of success.

The first part of action is the mental side. It's the visualization, seeing yourself accomplishing your goals. It's taking time throughout the day to think about what it takes to reach your goals. You are mentally walking yourself through a step-by-step process of what you need to do.

Again, this isn't to be confused with dreaming. This is a mental visualization, a mental walkthrough, if you will, of actual physical action. It's seeing yourself walk through the steps, one by one, and doing it over and over and over again. In the book, *The Strangest Secret*, the strangest secret is that you become what you think about. Buddha said the same thing way before *The Strangest Secret*. You have to think about what that means. You don't become what you dream about. You become what you think about.

If you want to be a successful businessperson, go to medical school, do well in high school, be the top salesperson at your company, or climb the corporate ladder, you need to mentally visualize yourself accomplishing those goals, but you also need to visualize yourself going through the process of getting things done. That's the first part of action.

This isn't theory. This is stuff that actually has worked for thousands of years since the beginning of time. The most successful people in the world use it. Professional athletes at the top of their game visualize themselves getting up to the plate and hitting that home run. They see themselves on the football field throwing the winning touchdown pass. Michael Phelps talked about seeing himself swimming for the gold medal. He visualizes himself winning that medal. Guess what? He's won a bunch of them. He's the most decorated Olympian of all time, and what does he do? He visualizes himself accomplishing the goals.

Mental action is something that you have to do day in and day out. If you just visualize yourself eventually being the CEO of your company, and you spend a lot of time one day thinking about it, it isn't just going to happen. You need to turn mental action into a habit. You need to persistently think about how you're going to accomplish that goal.

Habitual mental action is followed by physical action. That means actually doing something. That means getting off your ass and doing something. You start taking the physical steps to accomplish your goals. Let's say, again, that you want to be the top salesperson at your company. The only way you're going to accomplish this is to actually make the highest amount of sales. How do you do that? You get off your ass and sell harder, meet with more clients, and change your tactics. You do just a little bit more each and every day.

Every day you just do a little bit more, a little bit more, a little bit more. You're not going to go from the bottom salesperson to the top salesperson by thinking about it and then maybe making a couple sales the next day. You need to persistently take action, day in and day out. The most successful people in the world don't just take action for one day or for one week, or for one month. They consistently take physical and mental action day in and day out. The top ambassadors at my company CloiXonné aren't better than everyone else, they take action. Day in and day out.

If you look at the top salespeople within my organization, or within any organization, the top salespeople, nine times out of ten, always stay at the top. Zig Ziglar, one of the greatest salespeople in the world, tells stories of how he became one of the most prolific salespeople of our time. He talks about how, very early on in his sales career, he climbed the ranks and became the top salesperson within the organization he was with, selling pots and pans door-to-door, and what he did to do that. What he did was he took physical action.

When you consider why so many self-help and business books don't work, the reason is that as human beings, we are not able to take massive and immediate action. Consistently taking massive and immediate action and sustaining it day in and day out simply doesn't work. So many books and trainings mistakenly tell people to "Hit Em with the Hein" and go from zero to one hundred overnight. It's not a reality.

We are however able to take small baby steps, each day getting a little bit better, doing a little bit more, trying a little bit harder. Eventually, the science shows, it takes over sixty days for those habits, those physical actions that you're taking, to become nonvolitional, meaning that your body just does them. Your brain has been reprogrammed. From there on, you don't even need to think.

If you are a successful salesperson, and for sixty days you follow a course of action that you know works, then you no longer need to worry about maintaining that pattern, because it will always work. Again, that's why, if you look at the top salespeople at any organization, it almost seems that for them, it's too easy. People try to figure it out. What is this guy doing? Is he gaming the system? He's got to be cheating somehow. When you look at most of these top performers, however, that's not the case. They're taking physical and mental action, and they've been doing it consistently over time; it has become a habit. It has become a nonvolitional part of their DNA. Their brain has been programmed to take action.

It's like getting up in the morning. Most people just get up in the morning, grab a cup of coffee, get dressed, and they're like zombies. They drive to work and sit in their cube, doing whatever. They mindlessly make it through their eight-hour day and go home. The most successful people, the ones that really climb, are the people who have taken intentional mental and physical action every day and turned these actions into a habit.

After I wrote my first book, a person reached out to me and shared with me her goal of owning her own business, she said: "I realized I've been holding back, and I want to do something with my life. In fact, I have a plan. I'm going to start my own business.

I'm going to make something of myself. My husband and I have been talking about it for years, but we're actually going to do it. We're going to go out and take action. We're going to take the mental action, we're going to take the physical action, and we're going to move forward with this business idea that we've been thinking about for years."

We discussed at length, and about six months later, I reached back out and asked, "How's the game plan going? How's the new business? You making any sales?" They responded and said, "Well, you know, we haven't really done it yet. We haven't really taken that step yet." You know why? Because it's difficult to actually take that step. Looking at the big picture, it's too intimidating even to start. When I was a kid in high school or even college, and I had a big paper I had to write that was twenty-five pages long, I would call my mother and say, "Mom, this is so much work." My mother would say, "One page at a time." Building a business is the same; you have to take it one step at a time. You have to do a little more every day to get started, to take action, to succeed.

If you want to do something, go somewhere in life, or just go on vacation, the only way you can do it is by taking steps in order to move forward. You need to think about where you want to go. Maybe you are thinking about how beautiful it's going to be on the beaches of Aruba. Now what do you need to do? You need to book the vacation. You need to think about dates, you need to think about the plane, you need to think about the hotel, you need to think about how much money, and then you need to start doing stuff. You need to start saving the money, you need to actually book the hotel. You need to book the flight. That's action. Before that, you were mentally thinking about your vacation.

If you apply this process, you'll get to that island, you'll get to that happy place. You just have to do it. Right now you may be thinking, "Oh yeah, I know that. I get it. I understand." Well . . . Why aren't you doing it?

In order to really go down that path to true happiness, true freedom, and real success, you need to mentally start thinking about what it takes to get there, and start doing it.

Folks, I know it works, because I do it every day. The most successful people in the world do it every single day. We're not talking about dreaming. We're talking about mentally preparing for the future, and we're taking about physically doing the work. That's what it takes to achieve your goals.

THE PROCESS

If you have read my previous books, attended my seminars, or listened to my podcasts on The Alden Report, you know that I have been a salesman my whole life. Recently, with the launch of our vodka, Emory Vodka, I've literally been out on the streets selling door-to-door. I'm selling the product myself to go through and understand the process. That brings me in to what we're going to talk about next. It has to do with sales, but applies to pretty much anything in life.

As we were getting our sales process ready for Emory Vodka, one of the ways that we were innovating was by reaching out to the licensees, the liquor stores, the nightclubs, the bars; but we're reaching out to them at multiple touch points. We send a postcard, then follow up with a phone call. It helps the salespeople from the distributor side when they walk into the store. They're able to start that conversation, saying "Hey, did you get the postcard?" or "Did you get the phone call?" Sometimes the proprietor will say, "We got a phone call from these guys, Emory Vodka. What's it all about?"

We're refining the process. Every day things get a little bit better. Nothing starts out perfect, but you've got to start somewhere—that's what entrepreneurs do. Someone once said to me, "The light isn't always going to be green." The light sometimes never turns green, and the stars are not always going to align.

Everything isn't going to be perfect to start your business. But you've got to start somewhere, right? So you try, and you take action as well as you possibly can. That's where we're at in the process of making these outbound phone calls and sending these postcards at Emory.

This is direct marketing. This is the type of marketing that works and has worked since the beginning of time. If you look at political elections, candidates and their teams are doing direct marketing. People might call it grassroots, but I call it marketing that works. There is a lot of technology out there, with the Internet, e-mail, text messaging, and all the different social media platforms. They are all great and all evolving as marketing tools, but there are a lot of great marketing techniques that just work, and this is the one that we're talking about. Direct marketing is what works to generate sales.

After being a direct marketer for over 15 years, I started our company CloiXonné (www.cloixonne.com). I realized that I could help the average everyday person become an entrepreneur. Work the business part time. Leverage a direct marketing system and platform I built and make money. All without little or no risk. They could follow our systems, learn the ins and outs of being an entrepreneur and grow their own business. Essentially take away the fear and excuses people always cripple themselves with. Already, some of our ambassadors have started other businesses that have nothing to do with CloiXonné, other than the fact that our company taught these people how to become an entrepreneur. Plus, they are still actively ambassadors within CloiXonné making real money! It's a win, win for everyone.

NEVER PREQUALIFY

When I was talking to one of our salespeople about the process related to Emory Vodka, he said to me, "You know, Mike, I was looking at some of the establishments that we were calling on, and some of them—they're just not a good fit for Emory Vodka, so I'm not going to call them." I said, "Whoa. STOP THE CLOCK! Why aren't they a good fit?" "Well, you know, I've gone on Google Maps, and I've looked at where they're located. Our vodka is an ultra-premium, high-end vodka, and these places . . . just don't look like the types of places that we want to be selling Emory Vodka."

Business Building Tip

Never prequalify anyone, or any customer, ever.

You've heard the saying "Don't judge a book by its cover." Folks, that rings true every single day. When I first started sales, I was selling cars, and I tell you, this was an amazing experience. It was enlightening, it was humbling, and it was difficult. One of the things that I learned was you never prequalify a customer when they walk through that door.

Early in the job, I was standing in the showroom with another more seasoned sales guy. We see this young kid get out of his car wearing a baseball uniform. Before he even walked in, the sales-person next to me said, "I don't want this kid. I don't want to deal with some kid who's in a baseball uniform. He's got dirt on him, he looks like he literally got out of a baseball game." I agreed to talk to the kid.

When the kid walked through the door, he was holding a flyer that we had sent out on the Mercury Cougar. We had an entry-level Mercury Cougar. Payments were $199 a month, and that's the price that the kid wanted.

He says, "This is the car that I want, and this is the price that I want." I said, "Great. Let me show you this car," and we went to the back of the lot. We had a bunch of different Mercury Cougars, so after he looked at the car featured in the flyer, he fell in love with the more expensive Cougar, of course. I had shown him maybe the middle of the line, because as a young salesperson, I had prequalified him, thinking, "This guy can't afford the expensive Mercury Cougar. He doesn't have enough money to put down. He's in a baseball uniform. He's all sweaty, he's got dirt on him. There's no way he can afford this."

I told my manager the situation, and my manager said, "Does he like the other cars? Did you take him for a test drive?" I said, "Yeah. I followed the sales process."

I said to my sales manager "This kid can't afford the car. He's too young. He doesn't have the money." My manager wrote down four squares on a piece of paper, outlining the different pricing. He wrote down the price of the car on one square and the payments on the other. The payments were for the car that the kid wanted, not the one that he came in to see, the least expensive one. The payments had a $5,000 down payment built in. It's a lot of money in any day and age, for anybody, whether you're a millionaire, or whether you're a kid in a baseball uniform.

I presented the kid the options, and he said, "Mike, I really love the car, and I can probably even afford these payments, but I can't come up with $5,000. Would you take $3,500?" I went back to my sales manager, and I said "Hey. This kid likes the car, says he can afford it, but he only has $3,500." The sales manager didn't blink an eye and didn't even look at me when he said, "Here's what we can do. Go back to him at $3,700, and tell him we can do it at that payment, if he does $3,700." I went back to the kid and asked, "Can you do $3,700?" He said, "Sure."

We wrote the deal up, and lo and behold, he had great credit. He bought the car, and we got everything squared away. He drove off the lot, happy as he could be. The average commission on the cars at the time was probably about $150. I made $1,200 on that deal. The sales guy that was standing next to me didn't want to talk to him, because he was some young kid in a baseball uniform. Well, guess what? That cost him $1,200. Never prequalify! Always be open to the idea that this buyer might be the right fit, even if they don't seem right at first glance. Prequalifying is one of the most difficult habits to break, but recognize it and never do it. By breaking this habit you will be more successful in business.

WELL, I DIDN'T PREQUALIFY AND I WASTED MY TIME

There is a difference between prequalifying and qualifying. When you look at someone, or someone calls your place of business, or you show up for a sales call, your brain is processing the whole scene. If you haven't broken the habit of prequalifying, then your brain is prequalifying even if you think you are not. Which is a bad thing, as you are essentially making a determination without doing any digging. When you meet a prospective client or customer you should, however, qualify them when you have the opportunity. Ask them questions that will help you determine the best way to go about the process of selling or developing a relationship. I have spent countless hours, literally years off my life, with people to whom I will never be able to sell, but they have turned into friends, partners, and mentors. In developing a process by which you ask a series of questions you will not waste your time.

Business Building Tip

Develop a series of probing questions tailored to your business to help you qualify customers, so that you won't prequalify anyone. This will improve the customer's experience as well as your business.

BLUE COLLAR GUYS HAVE MORE MONEY THAN YOU

My good friend Kevin's dad, is a businessman, an entrepreneur, and he owns a machine shop. He is a classic blue-collar guy. He is your salt-of-the-earth, classic New England guy, someone you want to hang out with. He's also a multimillionaire. You'd never know it when you talk to him.

Kevin's father went into a Mercedes dealership a couple towns over. He was looking to buy two Mercedes Benzes, one for himself and one for his wife. He walked in wearing jeans and a T-shirt, and the salesman who greeted him asked, "Are you sure you can afford this? This is a 550 AMG Mercedes. This is probably about $110,000 car. Is it something you really—or maybe you should come and look at an E class." He was condescending and he prequalified my buddy's father, who was angry and immediately left.

The next day he came back. He knew exactly what he wanted. He walked up to a new salesman and said, "Come here, kid. You're about to make a big commission," and he bought two Mercedes Benzes. He went up to the other sales guy and said, "You should never prequalify anybody, kid."

Whether it's business or daily life, you never want to prequalify anybody. You never want to just say, "I'm not going to attempt to make that sale. I'm not going to attempt to make that phone call. I'm not going to attempt to talk to them, because they don't have the money. They're not able to do it." Those are the types of thoughts that lead to missed opportunities, and the types of people who act on those thoughts are unsuccessful. It's an easy mistake to make, but it's critical that you don't.

SCRIPTS WORK, TRUST THE PROCESS

In my call center at Blue Vase Marketing and CloiXonné, our internal sales agents naturally want to prequalify people, based on region, or the time of day they call, or the sound of their voice. To avoid these kinds of errors, we have a script. We build talking points into the sales process to overcome those natural instincts that some people may have to prequalify. Our agents follow the script. They read it with enthusiasm and trust the process.

We know it works. It doesn't give them the opportunity to prequalify anybody, and it increases their income. When you prequalify people, you're losing money. I know some of you might say, "It's a waste of time if I talk to so-and-so, or if I continue to talk to these people or that person," or whatever it is. You know what? You might be able to talk to somebody and realize, at some point, that you're not going to sell to them, but you would never know if you had just decided not to talk to them. Here are some basic probing questions you can ask a prospective client to see how serious the person is, or if you can do business:

1. *How did you find us?* This gives you some data on where they came from, was it an Internet ad you ran or a radio ad? Both are different ads and now you know how to tailor your discussion.
2. *Have you ever...?* Have they ever purchased your type of product or service before? This can help you understand why they have come to you.
3. *What sort of challenges are you having now?* This is a very broad type of question to see what their challenges are and how you can solve them.

These are just some examples of probing questions that help you qualify, but never prequalify, a prospective client or customer.

Never prequalify anybody for anything. If you keep that lesson as a tool in your tool belt, as a part of your arsenal in success, I guarantee that it will increase your success in anything you do in life.

CHAPTER 5

To Know and Not to Do

I was listening to Leo Buscaglia, a prolific speaker and author who passed away several years ago. He wrote the book *Love*. I'm told that he was the one who came up with that slogan, "To know and not to do is not to know." There are very important business and life lessons to learn from this phrase.

Business Building Tip

To know and not to do is not to know.

If you want to be successful, you have to have a plan. My plan was to build Blue Vase Marketing.

But to know your business plan, to know what you should be doing and to not do it, is to not know it.

There are a lot of you out there who know something, and you know how to accomplish something, but you don't do it. Maybe you know how to run a restaurant because you learned it. Growing up, maybe your family had restaurants. You started out washing dishes as a kid. Then you worked as a line cook. Then you were a waiter; later, you managed the front part of the restaurant. You've done it all, so you want to start your own restaurant. You know it. But you don't do it. That's one of the saddest things that I think happens to entrepreneurs. You know, but you don't do. So then you really don't know.

In Chapter 4, we talked about accomplishing your goal by taking action, both mental and physical action. Most people don't follow up with the second part of action. They know, they visualize, but they don't do. If you have a goal in mind, if you have some information that you want to share with people, and you know you want to get it out there and yet you don't—well, then, you really don't know. It's simple, but profound.

When I first became a lawyer I was working in a call center. One of the call center agents heard that I passed the bar exam, and asked me to represent him in his divorce. He was a nice guy, but he had just made a lot of bad decisions in his life. I took family law. I understood divorce. I looked at him like he was crazy. I said, "I just passed the bar exam. I can't do that. I'm not ready." He looked at me and said, "Mike, you've got to start some time." In that moment, I did know, and I didn't do it. When I look back at that interaction, there's a reason why I didn't—because it wasn't what I wanted to do in law and I was a little scared.

That request showed that I did know. I didn't take that step, because I was scared, just like you, just like so many people are. They're nervous. They're scared. They're scared to get started on accomplishing their goals.

If I had taken on that divorce case, I would have learned more. I would have learned the ins and outs, the practical side, of practicing family law. I felt I wasn't ready yet. Here's the thing: you're never going to be ready.

Business Building Tip

You're never going to be ready.

On the flip side, my heart wasn't really in it. A lot of people know things, but their heart really isn't in it. My heart's in this, writing this book; it's in Blue Vase and Cloixonné. This is what I want to do. I want to share what I've learned, the mistakes I've made, the tricks of the trade. I want to help you build businesses.

That's what I know, that's what I'm doing, and therefore, I know it.

Business Building Tip

Put your heart into it. Passion is an essential ingredient in business success.

My producer of The Alden Report said to me, "Mike, when you start talking on the microphone day in and day out, it's almost going to be like therapy for you," and that's absolutely the case. Sharing my mistakes and my triumphs with the public is like therapy for me. On my podcast I'm beyond candid with the listeners. I tell you about the mistakes I've made. I tell you about the things that I've learned. I tell you about where I'm going.

A lot of people don't buy into this stuff that I'm talking about. You know what? I didn't buy into this stuff either. To know and not to do is not to know. I used to hear people say that all the time. Who cares? I'm trying to pay my bills. I don't want to hear any of your bullshit. Right? How does this apply to my life? That's what some of you are probably saying right now. I've said that.

But when you think about successful people, the people you admire, you see that they're achieving their goals. They've found success by doing what they know. Follow in their footsteps. If you have something that you want to do, especially something that you know and love, go out and do it.

CHAPTER **6**

What Is Success?

In his book *The Strangest Secret*, Earl Nightingale says that success is defined as the progressive realization of a worthy goal. I think that's the best definition of success. The key is that it's a "progressive realization"; we have to tackle success on a micro-level, a small level. For instance, I consider writing this section of the book today a success. Focus on these micro-successes or micro-wins and compound on them throughout the day. We always have temporary defeats and minor losses throughout the day, but we also have successes throughout our day that move us toward our worthy goal.

I had the chance to meet and be interviewed by business mogul and *New York Times* best-selling author Grant Cardone on his show "Power Players" a few years ago, and he asked me how I defined success. My answer was exactly what I just said. The funny part of the story was that I fumbled through it and one of the camera guys helped me piece the quote together. Grant and I have similar yet also very different philosophies about business, but you cannot deny his success as he defines it. I was reading one of his blog posts recently in which he said something to the effect that he never wanted to be rich, but he always wanted enough money so that if he ever made a mistake in business it wouldn't matter or affect his way of life. He has met the progressive realization of that goal for all intents and purposes and I admire his drive and passion! If you're interested in what Grant Cardone has to say about success, check out my podcast The Alden Report. I ask him the same question.

Business Building Tip

Focus on the micro-wins that move you forward.

Success to you and to me are two different things. Some people believe that in order to be successful in life they need a nice car, a nice house with the two kids, the white picket fence, the dog, and the soccer mom. They're able to take a vacation once in a while. That very well may be success to you. You don't need to worry about what other people think as far as whether or not it's successful to others. It comes down to what you want and the goals that you set in your life.

Often people gauge their own personal success based on what they see in the media, what they see on television, and what they hear about the rich and famous. That isn't necessarily success for you. If that's something you want, if you want to be a box-office hit, or a successful singer, or an actor, or whatever your goal is, success is the progression toward a worthy goal. Each step that you take in the direction of that goal is also success. When you break down what Earl Nightingale said, it's really about getting there.

Business Building Tip

Define what success means to you.

Each day, day in and day out, as you accomplish things and you get closer to your goal, you are a success. That's it. It's not the millions of dollars in your bank account. It's not the nice watches, the nice cars, and everything else. It's the step-by-step, day-by-day, goal-by-goal progressive realization of success.

In the book *Outliers*, Malcolm Gladwell seeks out a definition of success. He looks at some of the most successful people throughout modern history. What's the key characteristic they all have? Every single one of them worked their ass off. Success isn't just given to someone. Success is something you work toward every day. You can't be afraid of that work.

In the United States we often demonize the successful people. We look at some of these rich people and we say, "They're bad people because they're so rich," or "They have everything that they want." They have everything that they want because they worked for it. Are there a few exceptions of people who hadn't worked that hard and are super-rich or "successful" in society? Sure. There's always an exception to the rule. Those are the ones that usually do fall off and don't maintain success, but the ones who really work hard are not afraid of what success brings.

The Beatles played for three hundred days a year for two years before anyone even knew who they were; they went on stage day in and day out. In *Outliers*, Gladwell talks about the 10,000 Hour Rule, which The Beatles personified. Basically, he says that in order be successful in whatever field you choose, you need 10,000 hours of deliberate practice to really become an expert and then, ultimately, become "successful" at it. *10,000* hours. That's a lot of hours of work. It doesn't happen overnight.

I see a lot of young people in this day and age who feel entitled, as though they deserve success. Why do you deserve success? Let's say you're twenty-seven years old, you're a couple of years out of college, you're working some job, and you're doing okay. What gives you the right or the sense of entitlement if you haven't worked toward the progressive realization of a goal? Now look. You can be very successful at twenty-two or nineteen years old. Again, look at the people who are micro-successes in college, high school, and middle school. You can be very successful on those levels, but you need to pay attention to those successes and compound on them.

There are many things you need to do and experience in order to find success: a lot of heartache, struggle, difficult times, and temporary defeats. That's the path you have to walk down in order to be successful.

EVERYTHING I TOUCH TURNS TO GOLD

A while ago, I was at a private beach here in Beverly, Massachusetts, talking to a friend I hadn't seen in a while. She pulled up in her Land Rover. She's pretty successful herself. So is her husband. I had told her about Emory Vodka. I said how well it was doing. She said, "Mike, everything you touch is gold."

That is the complete opposite of the truth. Most everything I try doesn't work. Look, it's difficult to talk about failure. It's difficult to wake up in the morning and be excited about that fact that something you put your heart and soul into, for which you put your best foot forward, didn't work. I like to call them temporary defeats something I learned from Zig Ziglar. I'm the type of person who doesn't like to give up on things. Sometimes there is a point where you have to realize the law of diminishing returns, that whatever it is you tried isn't going to work. It's okay to realize that. It's not giving up. It's realizing that maybe you need to step back, stop the clock, reevaluate, and go in a different direction. It's NOT failure.

Business Building Tip

Nobody wins every time, but in order to win, you need to stay in the game.

Often if the first thing you try doesn't work, something else comes of it. Emory Vodka started when I backed an artist, Blake

Emory. I love his art. I put him in galleries all over the country, Los Angeles, Boston, Miami, New York. His art has found acclaim, but financially it's still not working. I asked, "What else can we do?" So we launched Emory Vodka, which is doing well, but of course in these early days requires consistent work, constant hustle. I'm out there selling the stuff myself because I'm so excited about it. I want to learn more about the business.

As in any business, you need to learn the business from the ground up. That's what I'm doing because that's what I know works: understanding the business, learning about the business, growing the business, and then compounding on those micro-successes. That's really what success is. When you're trying to figure out what you want to do, what some of your goals are, what some of the things you want to accomplish are, set those goals. Work toward those goals.

Real, long-term success, the kind that builds legacies, takes a lot of hard work, heartache, and tough decisions, the decisions that most people won't make.

IS ALDEN ESSENTIAL?

I recently had a tough time making the decision of calling it a day with a particular advertisement that we created. It's an advertisement for our product called Alden's Essentials, an all-natural, vegetarian multivitamin offered by our sister company CloiXonné and it's selling well within CloiXonné. It's an awesome product, and I loved the advertising my team had pulled together.

Then we tested it. It did horribly on television. That's a gut-wrenching feeling, seeing something you love not work. Now we have to step back, look at the results, make tweaks, and see if we can improve it. At some point, it just might not work. Then we move on to the next thing. I'm not afraid of failing, but don't misunderstand me. Failing sucks. The human psyche feels it. Everybody feels it. You have to remind yourself that when you fail, a new door will open. Something else will come about as a result of it. Failure is part of the journey; I look at things not working as temporary defeats. Temporary defeats are learning experiences that ultimately will make you better. Alden's Essentials just didn't work on television, but it is doing extremely well in CloiXonné and helping people all over the world. One door closes another one opens.

FAILURE ISN'T FAILURE

Again, I like to call what many people call failures, temporary defeats, and it happens to everybody. It's part of the progressive realization of a worthy goal. Throughout that journey, you're going to have missteps. You're going to make mistakes. You're going to have things not go your way. I remind myself of that every day. Sometimes things aren't going to go your way, but if you truly have a goal and you want to be successful by accomplishing that goal, then you need to push forward. You need to recognize that things sometimes aren't going to go your way. In Chapter 8 we discuss failure in depth.

Business Building Tip

Remind yourself that sometimes things aren't going to work, and prepare to adapt.

The most successful people in the world work hard at accomplishing their goals. Don't be afraid to do the work to get there. Don't be afraid to climb to the top.

When you see successful people, ask yourself, "How did they get so rich? What did they do? What sort of goals did they set? What sorts of struggles did they have?" Internalizing the fact that success is the progressive realization of a worthy goal, and accepting that there will be multiple speed bumps and challenges along the way, will help you grow. When you put your heart into something and it doesn't work, there is no other way to describe it—it sucks! It hurts. It happens to me almost every day! But this is what entrepreneurs do. We keep pushing. Understanding this will not make the pain go away, but it will help you move forward.

WINNING THE LOTTO DOESN'T MAKE YOU A SUCCESS

I have a friend who hit $10 million on a scratch ticket. He was a police officer who hit $10 million on a scratch ticket. But he knows that money doesn't make him a success. He was a successful police officer. What will ultimately make him "successful" in life is what he does with that $10 million, how he manages it. He retired from the force, but he sought out a new line of work as a professional painter. A guy who hit for TEN MILLION is out there still working. His success will come from what he does with that money, and how he manages his time.

He loves fishing. He set a goal to become a professional freshwater bass fisherman and one of the top bass fishermen in New England. I asked him, "What's your goal? What do you want to do?" You see, even if you hit the jackpot, you need goals. You need some sort of benchmark. You need to know where you are. Ask yourself, "What's my endgame? Where do I need to go in order to be successful?"

My friend the lotto winner is working toward his goal of becoming a top bass fisherman. He's entered competitions. He's getting out there every day. He's learning about the ins and outs of fishing. He's discovering the science behind the types of lures, rods, boats, and the times of day. He's working toward that goal.

Just working toward that goal makes him successful because it's the progressive realization of a worthy goal. I don't know if Earl Nightingale would believe that worthy goal is becoming a professional fisherman, but whatever is a worthy goal to YOU is a worthy goal. It's not defined by what others think. You may read this and think that becoming a professional fisherman is a complete waste of time. That's fine, but that's a goal that he set. That's a goal that he's working toward.

Business Building Tip

Whatever is a worthy goal to YOU is a worthy goal.

I've started dozens of companies and grown them from nothing to entities generating millions of dollars. You know what? There's really no secret. There's no secret formula behind success, but there is a method.

There is a mental state, but there are certain fundamental things that you can do that most people don't do. You don't just become successful. It doesn't happen. You're not going to wake up tomorrow and be successful. If you truly want to take your business and your life to the next level, then internalize what you have learned in this book thus far and in future chapters.

It's not bullshit. It's not theory. It's not abstract thought. I'm not teaching a business class at a junior college and never been in business. I'm doing it right now. I continue to do it day in and day out.

CHAPTER 7

Opportunity

In the early 1970s there was a young man from Brooklyn, New York, who was fascinated with the music industry. He wanted to be in the industry in any capacity. He applied to work at multiple studios as a "sweeper." A sweeper was really just an assistant who would get the things recording artists and others working in the studio needed. This meant everything from providing alcohol or tea to actually sweeping up the mess that was made. It was a wild time, just coming out of the sixties. This young man, roughly eighteen years of age, grew up in a traditional Italian home. His mother stressed the importance of family and being together as a family. He was also taught the value of hard work and to be of service when asked for help. One fateful day the studio manager asked the young man to come in on Easter Sunday. His mother was not having it, and she instructed him to be home for Easter Sunday. He was conflicted, but he had learned to always be of service when asked. And so he decided to come to the studio. When he walked through the door on Easter Sunday in the early seventies, one of the most iconic musicians ever to walk this planet was sitting there to greet him. John Lennon himself. John and the studio manager wanted to see if this young man had what it took to work with John Lennon on his upcoming albums. That young man later went on to work as an engineer with John Lennon and the likes of Stevie Nicks, Patti Smith, Bruce Springsteen, Tom Petty, U2, Dr. Dre, Eminem, and many others. His name is Jimmy Iovine and he is the founder of Interscope Records. He recently sold the company Beats, a joint venture with Dr. Dre, to Apple for $3 billion. I heard Jimmy tell his story on *The Howard Stern Show*. He told the listeners and

Howard what got him to where he is today is that he is always of service to others.

Everybody loves the idea of being an entrepreneur, right? They love the idea of making money. They love the idea of making their own money. They love the idea of success. But they're not willing to show up. You have to be willing to be of service. You have to be willing to go through a rigorous process. You have to set goals, go after those goals, and accomplish those goals.

HOW TO SCREW THINGS UP

There's a way to really screw up an idea, a business, or an opportunity and it happens all the time. Aspiring entrepreneurs set intentions in their head, but they're never able to get out of their own way. That's one of the things that I found when I've been coaching people over the last few years. People ask me for advice and then they don't take it. Why'd you ask? If you're going to ask for advice you should not only listen, but you should actually take it as well. Listen and learn from those who have been there and done that.

Often people hear what they want to hear and hope that they'll get affirmation of their theories or their ideas, but in all reality it's just pie-in-the-sky type of thinking.

I want to get into the differences between an opportunity and a responsibility and how they come together. I have discussed this difference in both of my previous books, because it's important, especially in business. I hate to pick on the Y generation. But I've seen twentysomethings who feel as though they should just climb right to the top and all of a sudden be making six figures; it doesn't happen that way.

One of the reasons why the younger generation or some of these entry-level employees aren't able to break through is because they're unable to recognize what an opportunity is, not just in business, but in life. A responsibility is something that is given to you that you need to take care of. You need to take care of that responsibility whether it be in your personal life or your place of employment.

In most companies, there are org charts that assign certain responsibilities within each position. I hate org charts. They serve a purpose, but people get caught up in the fundamentals; they become so unable to think outside the box that they stick to this org chart thing. I think it can ruin companies as well as personal relationships when people feel as though their role is one thing and that's it. People are so focused on their assigned responsibility that they miss opportunities.

WHAT I LEARNED FROM 1-800-FLOWERS

The busiest time of year for florists is, of course, Valentine's Day. At 1-800-Flowers, the leading flower delivery service, they handle the massive call volume by having everyone, from the people in shipping to the CEO, take customer calls. Everyone pitches in to meet the business goals and deliver the best possible service. My former COO worked there, and he told me that's how they did it when they first started.

If you read my first two books, I briefly touched on this story and why it is so important. When I started Blue Vase Marketing, we were a small team and had an advertisement that just brought in a lot of interest. As we started to grow the team, we brought in a new accountant to help us manage the finances. The advertisement brought in so many calls that we needed help. We didn't have enough people to answer the phones.

As calls flowed in, I decided to try out the 1-800-Flowers approach; I asked everyone at the company to get on the phones, to make sales while the advertisement ran. Everyone did it, except my CFO/accountant. The next day my general counsel came to me and said, "Hey, Mike, did you notice Rich's office is completely empty?" I said, "No, I didn't notice." It was startling because this guy controlled my money. I called him at the end of a long day, while we were all still in the office. I called and he didn't answer. I called again and I said, "Rich, if you don't call me back you're fired." He didn't call me back.

At my companies Blue Vase and CloiXonné we don't stick to the org charts. We all have responsibilities, we all have titles, we all have roles, but we all also chip in when it's necessary—and that's what makes our company great and that's what makes a lot of other companies great. When we parted ways, I explained to Rich that I was giving him the temporary responsibility to jump on the phones and to take some sales calls. I just needed him to answer the phone, say hello, and sell some stuff.

He felt as though that it was beneath him. He said, "Mike, I'm a CPA, I've got my master's degree, I'm an accountant." I've learned throughout the years: your degrees don't mean anything. It doesn't matter, when it comes down to real business and the real world. People don't ask you, what did you get on your SATs or what was your GPA in law school? What did you score on the boards in the CPA exam? It doesn't happen.

Business Building Tip

Don't be beholden to your organization chart.

He says, "I'm a CPA, I don't feel as though I need to take sales calls." I said, "Rich, I gave you the responsibility to do this because I wanted you to learn more about our sales process as our accountant, as someone who handles the money. I was really giving you the opportunity to learn, to understand how we actually operate and what we do here at Blue Vase; maybe you could improve on the process. You see, your eyes are different from my eyes, Rich. You look at things differently than I do and maybe you could have improved upon things." Then I fired him. I fired him because he was unable to recognize that what I was giving him was truly an opportunity. I was giving him an opportunity to succeed.

Many people, day in and day out, are unable to recognize what an opportunity is. Most times an opportunity is wrapped up in a new responsibility. When you're given a new responsibility at your place of employment, a new responsibility in your personal relationships, look at it as an opportunity to grow, to learn, to do more things, to get better. Don't say to yourself, yeah I didn't go to school for this. This isn't why I went to school and studied, this isn't what I want to do. Rather, I'm working here now with this company, this great company, and this is an amazing opportunity to learn more about the company and how it operates.

Business Building Tip

Opportunity comes in the form of new responsibilities.

If you're working at a job that makes you feel unappreciated, as if you're just a number or a cog in a wheel, you may feel as though your boss doesn't care and it's just some big corporate empire and no one really knows anybody. That may full well be the case. That may be your reality, but one of the best ways to change that reality is to understand when you're given an opportunity.

Many times, opportunity is wrapped up in a responsibility. Let's say you're working at a fast-food restaurant, you're making minimum wage, and your job is to work at the fryolator making French fries. You were hired to make French fries. You did that at another place and that's all you know how to do.

At the end of your shift, your manager says, "Hey, I need you to help out on the grille and I need you to learn how to make hamburgers. We have a process here, and I need you to do it right now." Your shift is over, you're ready to go home. Now what do you do? If you have other obligations that you need to get to, you need to weigh those and take a look at this opportunity that has just been given to you. The opportunity that was given to you was to learn more about the business. It was a responsibility wrapped up in an opportunity, and the opportunity allows you to grow. It builds your own personal net worth. Now it's your decision to seize that opportunity.

Building your personal net worth will help your business. When you build your personal net worth, you become more valuable. You become more valuable to your employer, and you become more valuable to *other* employers.

LOSING ONE DEAL MAY LEAD TO ANOTHER

Recently I met with a representative of a distributor I was trying to land for Emory Vodka. I told the distributor that everyone I had presented Emory Vodka to in a different territory said yes to me. They wanted to see it for themselves and set up a meeting. Now, landing a distributor is huge for a brand as you can leverage their network and sales team. The guy I met with wasn't your average sales guy, he knows the distilled spirits business better than anyone I have ever met. I joked around and told him he has a PhD in distilled spirits. In his office, he showed me more about the process of distilling spirits. He had maps on his wall showing where ingredients come from and why they are good or bad for certain distilled spirits. He showed me spirits from all over the world, some I've never heard of. Even though I was learning from him, I was annoyed. I was there to sell him Emory Vodka and show him everyone wanted our vodka. I was not there for a lesson. I had already gone door-to-door myself and knew what I was doing.

I failed to recognize what was going on in this meeting, I was blinded by my ego and couldn't see the opportunity. I had to step back and say to myself, "Mike, this is an amazing opportunity." It wasn't a responsibility, he wasn't giving me anything to do, but I was given the opportunity to go out with this gentleman and learn from him. He was also giving me advice on our message and how to refine it. He taught ME about OUR process of distilling. This was an opportunity to build rapport with him and ultimately close the sale. He was giving me all this information, before we actually went door-to-door.

So after meeting with this guy for about an hour in the office, he was ready to take me out and see if what I was saying about our success held true in his territory. At first I didn't really like the sales process. I wasn't familiar with his sales process; it just didn't click with me. About an hour into our going door-to-door in hundred degree weather together it clicked. His process was designed to not only sell, but determining if there was genuine interest. His process was completely different than mine, but it worked. You have to trust the process of others who know more than you. If may not be immediately apparent, but if you are learning from someone else, trust the process. In this instance I was going door-to-door with an industry expert who knew a lot more than me. When I pushed him on why we were doing this he taught me a valuable lesson. He said, "Mike selling a bottle of vodka to a liquor store isn't that hard. Selling a bottle of vodka to a liquor store that will get behind it and help you sell it when you are not there is how you build a brand." This is true for all products and brands. Selling through product when you aren't pushing the product yourself or through your advertising is a key element to building a lifelong sustainable business.

I was being given an opportunity to learn about not only distilled spirits, but how they're sold, what my competitors are doing, some of the sales techniques that my competitors were using, what shelf space looks like, how liquor store owners react to things, and what they're looking for. When I realized that, I just wanted to slap myself and say, "Mike, this is an amazing opportunity."

You always hear people say you can turn a negative into a positive or turn lemons into lemonade. It sounds crazy, but there's almost always a silver lining to something negative. After spending all this time trying to close this distributor, they ultimately passed. I knew we were not a perfect fit, but I thought they would pick us up. When we were going door-to-door together every store did in fact say they would pick up Emory Vodka just like I told them. I assumed we would be doing business together. They liked the brand, they liked me, but in the end they referred me to another distributor who picked up Emory and is doing great things with the brand. The thing about opportunity is that it doesn't always come in the exact form that you wanted or expected.

Success doesn't just happen overnight. Obviously it didn't just happen overnight for me, and sometimes we need some retraining ourselves, we need a retooling, we need to go back to basics. Professional athletes practice every day. Last night I watched Tom Brady and the Patriots win their first game of the season. He's arguably one of the best quarterbacks in NFL history. Yes, he may have deflated the balls, or he may not have, but it doesn't matter. Here's how he became Tom Brady: he practices every single day.

He visualizes himself on the football field, throwing the touchdown pass, throwing it to Julian Edelman in the top right-hand corner of the end zone. Actually sees himself doing it. Then he physically goes out and does it. If you want to be the next Tom Brady, you're not going to get there from your parents telling you that you can be the next Tom Brady. You can't be the next Tom Brady unless you go out and do the things that Tom Brady does.

Since writing this section Tom Brady and the Patriots went on to win one of the most exhilarating games in Super Bowl history. Pulling off what some may have thought was impossible. Not for

Tom Brady and the Patriots. He prepared for virtually any situation including being down by several touchdowns in the fourth quarter of the Super Bowl and WINNING.

Whether academics, business, or relationships, we all need to work at it every day. The most elite and successful people in the world know this.

Too many people are given opportunities and they blow it, because (1) they can't recognize it, and (2) they were told by someone who isn't successful that it's just not the right thing to do. But it is the right thing to do. This is how successful people think, and this is how they progress. They question what they've been told; they think outside the box. This is how you get better in life: with your ability to recognize an opportunity and know how to take advantage of it. If you're given an opportunity wrapped up in a responsibility, you need to exploit it to your own advantage. Then you'll grow and prosper, and then your net worth will increase.

MORE THAN YOU GET PAID FOR

As a young lawyer working for a large company, I was very busy with contracts, transactions, and advertising. My boss asked me to look into something that was personal for his family. They were having some challenges with their neighbors, who were planning to build a deck that was going to ruin their shared beach.

As a lawyer, you don't know everything about the law, and I knew nothing really about real estate law. Sure, I took the class in law school as part of my curriculum, but I always found it boring. My boss's next-door neighbor happened to be a powerful real estate lawyer. She had filed a request with the town to build a giant deck that was going to encroach on my boss's property and ruin the beach, a beautiful place on an island in New England.

He asked me to look into it so I did. I learned about not only real estate law, but also maritime law because it had to do with a coastal area. I researched and I helped put together a very strong argument on why this deck should not be put in; it was a lot of fun for me to learn about. There was a lot of history there, and I discovered things I never knew. I did this in my off time and I wasn't paid for it. Legally, he couldn't even pay me for it. I wasn't technically representing him as an individual. I was just doing the research for him. I compiled the research, I wrote it up, handed it to him, and let him take it from there. He took what I wrote and used that as an argument with the town, and he prevented his neighbor from building this deck.

For me, obviously, that was a great win, but it was a lot of work. He gave me a pat on the back and said thank you very much, but this was early on in my career and I was maybe making $50,000 a year or something like that. When I left that company I was the highest-paid person there. I saw that new responsibility and knew it was an opportunity—to learn about maritime law and real estate law, but more important, I had a chance to show my boss that I was willing to go the extra mile. I was willing to take the time to learn, and I exploited the opportunity that was given to me.

I took advantage of the opportunity, which was, again, a responsibility and an opportunity. I wasn't paid for it, but ultimately I was, later on in my career.

What I want you to remember is that when you're given a responsibility, it's really an opportunity. At some point down the road—maybe not immediately, maybe not the next day, the next week, or next month—you'll find that your responsibility turned opportunity is truly going to increase your net worth.

CHAPTER **8**
Failure

I have never failed at anything.

Failure to me is fatal. When I think of failure, I think of something that truly has come to an end. That's all. It ended.

I tell people that I suffer temporary defeats every single day. As I said earlier I learned that from Zig Ziglar. If you don't know who Zig Ziglar is, I suggest you go online and buy all his books and audios. He changed my life.

When you look at some of the things that I have gone through, a lot of people would look at them as failures. The first time that I took the bar exam I missed it by one question. One question was the difference between passing and not passing. Not failing, but not passing. A lot of people say it's a pass/fail test and academia will tell you that you failed. If I truly had failed I would have given up and not gone back to take the bar exam and pass. Failure, again, is fatal. It's something that you've ultimately just given up on. When you start to change how you think about failure, to consider things not going as planned to be a temporary defeat, your mindset starts to change.

When I didn't pass the bar exam, friends expressed their concerns for me, saying, "Mike, I'm sorry that you didn't pass and it's really too bad. A lot of people don't pass the first time. It took JFK Jr. five times to pass the bar exam." None of that made me feel any better. I didn't look at it as a failure. The biggest thing I learned from that experience is that I wasn't prepared.

In my book, *Ask More, Get More*, I talk about how you can mitigate and prevent failure to stop the negativity that comes along with it. I wasn't prepared the first time for the bar exam. I only studied for a few weeks, and it's the type of exam that you need to study for dozens of weeks. The second time I took it, I passed. The second time I felt as though I knew more about the law than I would ever know and I was prepared to go in. I also wasn't afraid to fail.

There are two options, right? There is success and then there's failure. Now there is no such thing as a failure gene or a success gene. For those of you who believe that people are born with something, that there's a genetic predisposition to success or entrepreneurship, you're wrong! Science has proven that's not the case. There's no such thing as a failure gene, and there's no such thing as a success gene. You can't use that as an excuse for why you're not doing well, why you're where you are in life, why you're not where you want to be, and things like this.

When we look at failure, we say to ourselves, "Well, I had this task that I was trying to achieve, but it didn't happen. I didn't get there. I didn't accomplish my goal." Instead of failure, call it "temporary defeat"; using this tool, your mind is able to program itself and move forward much more easily. Often people are afraid to fail. You think, "I don't want to fail. I'm afraid to fail. I don't want to seem like a failure." Because that's what you always hear when you're younger, "You don't want to be a failure in life." You don't want to disappoint your parents, your teachers, or your family. Don't be a failure. Right?

You're programmed as a young child to be deathly afraid of failure. Now, there's nothing wrong with fear. I think fear is a good thing. It drives a lot of people. Where most people screw up is when they're afraid to fail to the point that they can't take action. You can fear failure. You can fear it, but don't be afraid to take the step that could possibly lead to a temporary defeat and not a failure. You see the difference there? You can fear it—in your head. You may be thinking, "I don't want to fail. I don't want to suffer a temporary defeat," but it's okay. Don't be unwilling to take that step to move forward and possibly suffer a major temporary defeat. That is the key.

The most successful people in the world fail every single day. Some of them are the true definition of failure. They're done. It's a fatal mistake in whatever venture they were attempting, but they move on. The most successful people have programmed their minds to recognize that what most people call a failure is a temporary defeat, and they are able to move past it. I ran into an old friend, and I was talking about some of the things that we have going on here at Blue Vase Marketing. I talked about one of our business ventures that I'm so excited about called "draftdemons.com." It's a daily fantasy sports website that's creating a lot of buzz in the daily fantasy sports world. It didn't work for us and we sold it. Is that a failure? No, we were defeated in the game we tried to play in, so we decided to play in another game.

When most people think of failure, they think of it in the traditional sense. They think of it truly as the end. When many people think of something as a failure, it becomes ingrained in their brain. It gets worse, and it continues growing like cancer until it has taken over your whole thought process and paralyzes you. I talk about Excusetosis in *Ask More, Get More*. It's one of the most prolific diseases that are out there. That's our minds making excuses for ourselves; failure happens the same way. If you look at failure as a fatal thing, as the end, as something that you just cannot overcome, and you have really disappointed everybody, and you consider yourself a failure, what does that do to your confidence? It destroys it. If you look at a brain scan, there is an actual chemical and physical reaction to every emotion and every thought that you have. These negative thoughts produce chemicals in your brain and body that are toxic, and they can continue to get worse.

When you look at people that society would deem failures, and do a brain scan or a body scan and test their blood, their systems would have chemicals and toxins that successful people don't have. When you scan people who are having positive emotions, their brains are filled with things like oxytocin and serotonin, chemicals and hormones that are released when you're happy. If you scan negative people who consider themselves failures, their brains are not smooth, meaning the actual gray matter our brain is made up of is rough and has jagged edges. They look all rocky, like the bottom of the ocean. It's a mess. Healthy, happy, successful people, their brains are smooth and rounded the way our brains are supposed to look.

If you consider yourself a failure, your brain actually manifests physical changes. When we talk about addiction, you hear people say, "Once an addict, always an addict." They say this because addiction is in your brain, chemically and physiologically. Certain things happen when you do drugs. You alter the chemistry of your body. You can do the same exact damage to your brain and to your psyche, if you believe that you're a failure.

So many people live their lives like this, day in and day out.

GRADUATE LAW SCHOOL AND DON'T TAKE THE BAR EXAM? REALLY?

In the face of hard circumstances and challenges, most people are paralyzed by the fear of failure. Paralyzed. Imagine a person who has wanted to be a lawyer their whole life. They first go to undergraduate school. Four years. Okay? Then they go to law school. Four years, depending on how you did it. All that's great. Then to truly achieve their goal, they have to actually take the bar exam. Then they don't pass the bar exam, but at least they got that far. That's what happened to me the first time. But others go through all this schooling and are so paralyzed that they don't even decide to take the bar exam! I went to law school with people who decided not to take the bar exam, they were paralyzed by the fear of failure.

At the end of the day, who cares if you fail? The only person who really cares, and should care, is you. If you go take that test, or if you move forward with the initiative that you've been thinking about for years, and it doesn't work the first time, is that a failure? To some people, it is. Now you know better: it's just a temporary defeat.

Folks, this stuff works. I know it works, because I do it every single day. It's difficult to think about, but it's not difficult to do. We hear a lot about the power of positive thinking, which is very important. But it's not the be all and end all, okay? It is one step forward in the right direction. If you reprogram your mind, you tell yourself you're not afraid to suffer a temporary defeat. Wouldn't you rather have tried? Wouldn't you want to at least give it a shot?

Often entrepreneurs suffer a temporary defeat and call it a failure. They could have gone into that same scenario and been successful at it, but they didn't do something that's really key to success in general. They didn't prepare. Go back to my bar exam scenario. I was not prepared the first time around. I just wasn't. I'd also begun to reprogram my mind, to understand that it was not a failure. In my office I have the letter that I got from the board of bar overseers that begins, "We regret to inform . . . " I keep it to remind myself that if I had looked at that letter and called it a day, that would have been the ultimate failure and I would not be where I am today.

Business Building Tip

Always prepare.

When you think about failure and success, the first thing you need to think about is yourself. It doesn't make you selfish. After all, what we're really talking about is you. We're talking about your brain, your thoughts, and your success.

The takeaway from this chapter is to no longer fail at anything. Again, I tell people that I've never failed at anything in my life. Doesn't it sound like such bullshit? It sounds so ridiculous, so overly confident and cocky. I suffer temporary defeats. Every single day I suffer temporary defeats, but I've never failed at anything. When you start to program your brain that way, things start to happen for you. You're able to work through the temporary defeats in a different way than you would have if you had considered them failures. You're able to see things just a little bit differently, and then people around you can see them that way too.

Like a disease, your attitude and the way you think about things does infect others. When you look at successful people, organizations, and families, you'll find they think just a little bit differently than most other people. That's really what it comes down to. Thinking just a little bit differently.

My second book, *5% More*, was really an accomplishment not only for me personally, but for my whole organization. We not only felt good about the book, but we felt great about the possibility of achieving our goal of producing a *New York Times* best-selling book. We sold thousands of copies of the book and from what I know about book marketing, we sold more than enough to hit every book list. BUT we didn't. Now, I'm not going to lie to you and say I was elated and happy because we had a great book and missing the *New York Times* was no big deal. It was a very big deal and it hurt. However, *5% More* has achieved some great things, and as I write we are continuing to change people's lives. Did it hurt? YES. But, just because we didn't hit that goal, it is certainly not a failure. Hard to see sometimes, but when you have trained your brain like

I have to recognize the good things even in not so good moments, what you used to consider a failure is in fact another opportunity.

Whatever It Takes

I was embarrassed to tell you the real story of how I bought my first bike in my earlier books. I told a story about how I bought my first bike with the help of my Uncle Buddy. I sugarcoated the story a bit. This is what I really did. At a very young age, I climbed into dumpsters looking for cans. I went through people's trash for cans and walked the streets with a large black trash bag to redeem at the redemption center. As I write, the feelings of shame are coming back to me. But it gets worse. I remember one summer being down at the local beach with a big trash bag going through trash cans. I remember the smell of trash and rotting food, and the sound of bees swarming around. Being dirty was difficult enough, but one time as I climbed back out, I saw a couple of kids I went to elementary school with. It was beyond embarrassing, and those kids looked at me like I had three heads. I still know those same kids, and they are all doing nothing with their lives. They were from upper-middle-class families and never really got an opportunity to understand the struggle. I feel sorry for them. Why do I tell you this story? This is what it takes to be an entrepreneur. You have to get dirty, you have to suck up your pride, and you have to do more than others. Now, nobody likes this feeling. Nobody really wants to put himself in that position, but when you see all the memes on social media about the iconic businesspeople of the world, they all have very similar stories. In order to be successful as a businessperson, you need to do whatever it takes. If you aren't willing to

(continued)

(*continued*)

commit to that, then stop reading and go back to the life you are living. But if you are willing, the rewards are beyond gratifying. When I rode my bike down the street when I was a kid, after I sucked up my pride, literally got dirty, and did what it took to buy that bike, the wind in my face going down a hill on a hot summer day never felt so good.

CHAPTER 9

Do What You Say

In business and in life, always do what you say you're going to do. Keep your word. When you tell yourself that you're going to do something, and you don't do it, you're doing yourself a disservice, and you're setting yourself back. The easiest person to lie to is yourself. People do it every single day. Not following through on something you said you were going to do is an absolute travesty. It's a travesty not only for you individually, but also for the people around you.

IN BUSINESS

What do successful people do? They do what they say they're going to do. One of my biggest pet peeves is when someone says, "Mike, I'm going to get this done for you, and you're going to have it on Monday at 9 a.m." Well, if you tell me that you're going to have something done for me Monday, at 9 a.m., when should I expect it? I should expect it at 9 a.m. The challenge is that in corporate America and people's personal lives, people fall short. They over-promise and underperform.

If you say you're going to do something, or provide a service, or be somewhere, or produce something at a particular time, make sure the time you give is accurate. Make sure that what you've promised is accurate as well.

People talk about a valuable final product (VFP), right? If you tell me, "Hey, Mike, I'm going to get you your book cover tomorrow," even though tomorrow is Saturday, and then, "I'll get it to you 10:00 tomorrow," what am I expecting? I'm expecting that I'm going to get it at 10:00 tomorrow. I'm also expecting that it's going to be what you said it's going to be. There are three components to that.

First, it's doing it when you say you're going to do it; second, it's how you say you're going to do it. So many people fall short of both. Third, when you overpromise and underperform, it ruins your credibility. It's very difficult for you to overcome that giant mistake. How do you avoid making that mistake?

HOW NOT TO OVERPROMISE AND UNDERPERFORM

You're at your job, and your boss says to you, "I'd like this report. I'd like it to be twelve pages long, I'd like it to have a detailed analysis of our profit and loss, and I'd like for you to give it to me at 9 a.m., Monday morning." You get this at 5:00 Friday afternoon. You know you're going away and can't get to it. Your boss repeats, "I need it at 9 a.m. Monday morning," but you know that it's not possible for you to get that done.

What do you do? You could just "yes" your boss to death and act like a go-getter. You can say, "I'm going to get that for you. Absolutely, Mr. Whoever," or "I'm going to get that for you, no problem. 9 a.m. Monday morning." But you know that you can't. And even though you know you can't, you just told your boss that you can. Now you have put yourself in a real predicament.

So how do you avoid this situation? Most bosses who know how to run a business are able to work around other people's schedules. They're able to overcome challenges, and they can handle it. You say to your boss, "Look, I don't know if you remember, sir, but I have to be out of town this weekend with my family. It's important to me. My family's important to me," which it should be. "I'm not really going to be able to dedicate a lot of time over the weekend; however, I know this is important, and I know that you need this in order to move forward with a business transaction. What I can do for you is I can get it to you by noontime on Monday. Would that work for you?"

Business Building Tip

Be clear and realistic in the promises that you make.

Now, forget about all the other whacked-out things that could potentially happen in this scenario. I know some of you are thinking, well, my boss is crazy, he's going to tell me I'm fired, or whatever you think may happen. What I'm really trying to tell you is you can prevent a withdrawal in what I like to call the Emotional Bank Account. You can prevent that by just giving your boss a realistic expectation. That's what your boss really wants. I'm a big fan of Chris Farley and in one of his best movies, "Tommy Boy," he plays the son of Tom Callahan, Tommy. He's a bumbling fool. He hits the road to try to sell auto parts for his dad's company. Tommy is a real mess and lacks basic skills to communicate. But after watching his father and hearing a few pep talks he starts to get the hang of sales. In one scene he is at a factory trying to sell the owner Callahan brake pads (Tommy's dad's product). The owner mentions a competitor and comments that Callahan doesn't have a guarantee on its box. Tommy rebuts a couple times but closes the sale by saying the product he is selling is a quality product and that anybody can put anything in a box with a guarantee on it. What matters is what they deliver on and how they stand behind the product.

If you say you're going to do something, you need to actually do it. You won't always be able to deliver at a requested time, but give them a realistic expectation of when it can be done. People like me, who build businesses from zero to hundreds of millions of dollars, are able to work through that. We get it. It's not always going to work properly. Things are going to get screwed up here and there. The difference between successful people and unsuccessful people is that the unsuccessful are overpromising and underperforming. You don't do what you say you're going to do. Business people respect honesty and open communication. Being up front, open and honest will get you on the successful track.

I have one business rule that you should follow when using a third party. I only require two things from a service provider. First, a product that works and does what they say it will do. This applies to actual products and services. Second, I require customer service. Even though the company sold you on the benefits of their product and how amazing their product is, things break. I require top-notch customer service from the ground up. If the CEO is willing to give you his cell phone number and answers when you call, that is a great indicator of how much they care about you.

IN PERSONAL LIFE

Always do what you say you will in your personal life as well. I'm a dad of an 11-year-old little girl. I don't believe there's ever been a time when I have said I was going to do something for my daughter and not done it. That's got to be the first thing, the first priority in life. Family comes first. Right? That's what people always say. There are some caveats to that, but look, if you make a commitment to a family member that you're going to do something, especially if it's your child, do it. Lead by example and show them that your word matters.

PARENTS, STOP OVERPROMISING!

I heard a story once about a little girl who used to wait for her dad on the weekends, standing there in her driveway for hours because he said he was going to be there, and he never showed up. To this day, she doesn't have a relationship with him. In your personal life one of the biggest things that you can do to hurt your relationship is to tell someone you're going to do something and then you don't do it. I am not a relationship expert when it comes to spouses. I'm divorced, but I've seen a lot of things, and I've seen a lot of people fail and screw up, and I try not to repeat some of the things that some of those people have done. Again, I'm not perfect. When you say you're going to do something, you have to do it.

What else can you do to make sure that you're not overpromising and underperforming? Don't commit yourself to things that you can't do. If you tell your daughter you're going to be at her soccer game, you need to be there. You need to be there! Look, like I said, there are instances where things just happen. I get that—things just happen. But if you tell your children that you're going to do something, you need to do it.

I'm talking about the real important stuff. I'm talking about when you tell your kids that you're going to read them a story tonight. Or you're going to help them with their homework. I'm talking about the real stuff that builds character. Human beings really thrive on emotional responses from one another. Try your absolute hardest to do what you said you were going to do.

SPOUSES

You can take that same story to the next level when it comes to your spouse. You say you're going to do something and you don't do it, and it comes down to the most basic, ridiculous things. You say you're going to take the trash out, and you don't take the trash out. It drives people crazy, if you say you're going to do the dishes or another chore, and you don't do it. Again, what I've been saying since the beginning is you need do what you say you're going to do, and then ultimately you will be successful in whatever that is.

If there are constraints or a challenge with a commitment you have made, you need to let the person know of that challenge. Now, what else can you do? What if things just totally go wrong? You've committed to something, you tell someone this is what I'm going to do, and it doesn't work out. For whatever reason. You've tried your best. You communicate the challenge and work through it. Not talking about it in your business and personal life can cause tension and erode the relationship.

BACK TO BUSINESS

Business involves human beings and personal relationships. Separating the two is difficult. This section will help. We are social beings, and many of our close business relationships are developed out of a personal relationship. When the two worlds collide it can be difficult to navigate.

Trust but Verify

Ronald Reagan, the fortieth president of the United States, was famously quoted as saying we should "trust but verify" when dealing with the Russians. Ironically, it's a Russian proverb that Reagan learned and then adopted into his political philosophy for dealing with the Russians. In business, especially when you are the CEO or have subordinates, you need to trust but verify constantly. I have personally made many mistakes by trusting what an employee said to me or a business associate told me. These mistakes have cost me millions over the years. Most recently I bought a business that a former friend of mine had started. I trusted him, I loved him like a brother. He was a hustler and a hard worker, and very knowledgeable about the business I purchased. The business was undercapitalized and that's where I came in. I helped fund the business so that it could thrive in the future. The challenge was that the business was in a different state, and I couldn't be there or easily send my trusted executives there daily. I did send my executives a couple times, and I had weekly calls, but I made the mistake of trusting too much. I trusted what he told me and took his words at face value. I never verified. That mistake cost me over $500,000 and a friendship. I had to shut the business down. My former friend got very upset with me, but he knew at the end of the day that he wasn't accomplishing what he had told me. Was he lying to me? Not completely. He just wasn't forthcoming with the information needed so that I could make informed decisions and even help him. Whether it is a large organization or a small one, whether you're the CEO or a mid-level manager, you have to verify and verify often.

Business Building Tip

One easy way to verify inside an organization is to do what your employees or subordinates do. This will give you a better idea of what is going on, and you'll get a view from their perspective and an opportunity to maybe improve the process.

THE VALUE OF CONNECTION CAPITAL

A good friend of mine, Larry Benet, calls the relationships he has built, Connection Capital. He means the connections between your relationships and the capital in those relationships, and how you build those relationships in a way is the most valuable currency there is. But he values those relationships on a personal level. He genuinely cares about the people he has a connection with. One of the ways you can hurt those relationships is by not doing what you say you're going to do. Now, again, we've all done it. I've done it. There have been instances where you just made a mistake.

What do you do when you can't deliver on what you said you would do? What do you do when you make a mistake? You have the best intentions, you forecasted things out, you prepared, and everything went haywire. Things just didn't work out the way you wanted them to. What do you do? First, you need to acknowledge it and let the other side know. Avoiding it is the absolute worst thing you can do. I've done it. I've avoided it. I've owed people millions of dollars, and having to pick up the phone to tell them that I can't pay them $2,000, when I owe them a million, is not a fun phone call to have. It's not a fun phone call, but that connection capital, that relationship that we've built and fostered, has taken years to develop, and it can evaporate very quickly. It will happen almost immediately if you don't acknowledge that their expectations are not going to be met and that you cannot do what you said you were going to do.

There's always going to be something that is going to come up. That's business. That's life. It's not always perfect. In fact, it's never perfect. You need to acknowledge it. Not acknowledging it will destroy your credibility and can destroy your connection capital. Your relationship capital can be demolished.

Among the things that have ultimately made Blue Vase and CloiXonné successful are my relationship capital and my connection capital. I started Blue Vase with nothing. Really, with nothing. Maybe $25,000 or 30,000 in credit cards, and the only other thing that I really had was my relationships. People always talk about, "your word is your bond." Most of that doesn't mean anything. Or you sign a contract? People always sign contracts. Contracts are important in business, but as soon as you have to look at the terms of the contract, you're in trouble. If you start having to look at the terms, there's usually something really, really wrong. Contracts are designed to lay out the terms of the negotiated deal. They lay the ground rules for the deal. But there are also terms and provisions that lay out what will happen in the event of say nonpayment, or some material breach. Despite the fact that I'm a lawyer and have written and negotiated hundreds of contracts, contracts should never have to be looked at after the deal is in place. When you have to look at the terms it means something is wrong with your relationship.

Sometimes things aren't going to work out the way you want them to, but if you don't address them your relationship capital can be destroyed, and your business can ultimately be destroyed. Often small vendors and new businesses are functioning paycheck to paycheck. If you can't pay or can't deliver, it hurts them. It hurts their business, their personal life, and their personal bank account. At the end of the day, there are humans behind every business, even in the world we live in today. There is always a human tied to a business.

I know what it's like to have somebody not pay you or have people not do what they say they're going to do. Most businesspeople can accept it as a hiccup in cash flow and understand things don't always go as planned. Communicating with your vendors is very important, because if they don't know what your challenge is, then they can't make a decision. If you give someone the information, "Hey, look, I can't pay you today," that businessperson, or whoever is on the other side, is then going to have to sit there and think, well, how do I fix this? How do I solve the problem that I have? Maybe I can go out and talk to somebody else. Maybe I can get a quick short-term loan. Whatever it is.

Get out ahead of this by letting them know where you stand and how you can remedy the situation. By doing that, you're giving them the ability to solve the problem. They can look elsewhere for budget, funds, or resources. If you've buried your head in the sand and you don't say anything, that businessperson is not able to make decisions. They're not able to move forward. They're not able to think things through. This is what we do as humans. We try to figure things out. You can't figure things out without the information. If you can't do what you say you're going to do, and you have the best intentions, then you need to let the other person know.

A LITTLE MORE ON DEBT

All of my vendors have given us terms over the years, meaning they give us time to pay once we receive a product or a service. Throughout the years, due to market conditions, growth explosions, or unforeseen constraints on cash flow, we have had to extend the terms originally granted from our vendors. No one likes this, especially the businesses we owe money to. However, even if you have to extend the terms essentially without their consent due to the reality that you can't make the payments as originally promised, your relationship is what keeps everyone calm. There have been situations where I've owed vendors hundreds of thousands and even millions. When you are generating millions then you are spending millions, and a hiccup one week could have an adverse impact on your business and thus a rippling effect on all those involved. Some of our relationships have changed over the years as people change jobs or businesses get sold. This is a precarious situation to handle, especially if you owe them money. Your relationship hasn't developed with the new people. It is tough to start a relationship when you owe a business a lot of money. If they are providing you a service and making money but you are in the hole, it's actually a great position to be in. I don't like being in this position but it is in fact a strong position. If the vendor decides to stop selling you their product or service, then they know it is a very real possibility that they will never get paid. That is just business. Now in my almost ten years at Blue Vase that has very rarely happened. The one time it happened was because the vendor had harmed me irreparably and it was my only recourse short of suing them. Always try to adhere to the terms of your original deal, but business is business, as they say, and if you have solid relationships they will work with you and help you grow.

Following are some business tips about debt:

1. If you are in debt, don't get too nervous.
2. Do your best to manage the debt by not pushing too far.
3. Recognize that if you owe a business money, and they are making money from your business, then you are actually in a good spot.
4. Communicate, communicate, communicate.
5. Be honest about your situation.

IF THINGS GO SOUTH

Sometimes business relationships fall apart. As an attorney who has represented clients in legal disputes, I know that things can go drastically wrong and get real nasty fast. One big reason why is a breakdown in communication and lack of proper connection capital building. When I practiced law I did my best to avoid lawsuits or get them settled as quickly as possible, as no one wins in lawsuits but the attorneys. I was general counsel, so I was being paid regardless of when I was practicing law. I learned early on that if you can get comfortable with losing, then you will be in an enviable position. That is, if you do whatever you can to avoid a lawsuit or salvage a relationship and it happens anyway, then get comfortable with losing. Anything in between is a win. As an attorney, I have used this idea—letting the other side know we are comfortable with losing—as a negotiating technique. It baffles people. But if people know that now you have nothing to lose, you have gained strength.

A little while ago, I had to renegotiate a contract that had unforeseen provisions in it that were costing my company tens of thousands of dollars a month that we should not have been paying.

We didn't see how this deal could go wrong for us, but it did. Contractually we were just locked in with zero leverage. I went to the other side and explained how this section of the contract was hurting us. They were not very empathetic toward our position. Now, this is a company I have connection capital with, but they are huge and my main contact had left. So my capital wasn't as strong. After trying to get them to remove the provision that was costing us tens of thousands each month, I explained that I may have to stop paying altogether. As a lawyer and a businessperson, I knew what this meant. It meant I was inviting a lawsuit. But I had gone through all the steps of trying to avoid that, and it wasn't going well. Let me be perfectly clear: we would lose in a contract dispute. That's just where we were. Ultimately after my meeting and some back and forth, the company was willing and able to reduce my contractual obligation in half! Remember, I had zero leverage. Well some would think that. What I had was a comfort level in the worst case scenario.

SOMETIMES YOU HAVE TO SAY "WHAT THE FUCK"

This phrase was classically depicted in the eighties movie "Risky Business" featuring a young Tom Cruise. The first time it was said was when Cruise's friend Herbert (Curtis Armstrong) tells Cruise that sometimes you have to say, "What the fuck." Herbert goes on to say that this phrase gives you freedom, freedom gives you opportunity, and opportunity is your future. I have been involved in some high-level negotiations in my career involving millions of dollars and people's lives, both as a lawyer and as a businessperson. When you are able to analyze a situation and think about what the worst case could be, and then be comfortable with it, this puts you in an enviable negotiating position. As a lawyer representing companies, I've had clients on the brink of forced bankruptcy with little to offer to settle. Sometimes my only option was to say, "What the fuck" (with the clients' consent, of course). When you can get comfortable with the worst case, you will find your position of strength and opportunities will arise. I've been involved personally as a CEO in scenarios where I owe others a lot of money and they aren't happy. Things happen. I've never gone into a deal intending to owe anyone money. But there is freedom, as Herbert said, in saying this phrase (what I really say is "Fuck it." If a business or a person is trying to force you into a situation that you are not able to be in, and they threaten consequences that could hurt you, letting them know you are comfortable with that really shakes them. Now, avoiding these types of situations at all costs is the best practice, but business is tricky and unexpected things happen, and many times not in your favor. Here is the moral of this story distilled down a bit. If you are in a tight spot, analyze the worst-case scenario, get comfortable with it, and then if necessary let the other party know it—only if you have to. But you must truly be comfortable with the worst case. It is liberating, fulfilling, and empowering all at once. No matter the result, you still win, and in most situations opportunity will arise.

Business Building Tip

When negotiating, try to look into the future and anticipate what may happen.

JUST DO IT

A couple years ago I came across Art Williams, the man who built A. L. Williams, one of the largest insurance companies in the world, now called Primerica Financial Services. He was a football coach turned entrepreneur who generated billions of dollars in revenue and made the Forbes list of billionaires. He gave a great speech in 1987 in front of the National Religious Broadcasters of America. The speech is called "Just Do It" and was given one year before Nike launched their iconic Just Do It marketing campaign. Art Williams is a masterful orator with a southern drawl that just makes you smile. I listen to this speech almost every day. The overarching theme in the speech is, you guessed it, Just Do It! You say you are going to lose weight—great, just do it; you say you are going to start a business—great, just do it; you say you are going to be number one in sales—great, just do it; you say you are going to be a millionaire—great, just do it.

My dad recently came to me to let me know he was thinking about going to Italy. Now, my dad works for me and he has complete freedom. Why? Well, he's my dad. Oh, and he makes a great wage. He told me he was thinking about going. I asked him what there was to think about? He told me money was a concern, timing, what to do with his dog and every other reason why he "couldn't go" to Italy. I looked and him and said look Dad, you only have so many days left on this planet, if you really look closely you have plenty of money, your "job" allows you to do what you want, so JUST DO IT! Whatever it is you are planning or want to do, just do it!!!!!

I'M GOING TO KICK YOUR ASS AFTER SCHOOL

Growing up I heard this threat a lot; I was in probably over fifty fights. I've always been a big kid, so people wanted to just challenge me to a fight. I never liked starting a fight unless I felt as though it was preemptive and necessary. I will always remember one morning when I was a sophomore. A bully in my high school came up to my locker as I was entering the combination, 19 . . . 37 . . . 13 (that is the actual combination). He told me in more colorful language that he was going to beat me up after school. Now, even though I was a big guy I was afraid of this kid. He wasn't playing with a full deck. I finished getting my books and, literally shaking, I turned and looked at him and said, "Let's do it now." He got in my face, but I stood there and said, "Let's just do it now. I have things I need to do later." I want to tell you that I triumphantly dropped him and just walked to class. But what really happened was that my response scared him. LET'S DO IT NOW! It crippled him. He didn't know how to react. He never bothered me again; in fact, he tried to befriend me. In business and in life, many people tell you they are going to do something, then plan to do something, and they never do it. They never do it because they are afraid of getting their ass kicked. Sometimes you will in fact get your ass kicked and it may hurt. But entrepreneurs know that and they push forward. Do whatever it is you want to do now. Tomorrow may never come and the future is uncertain, so LET'S DO IT NOW! When I wanted to go to law school, I did it; when I wanted to get my license to carry a firearm, I took the class and applied; when I wanted to backpack through Europe, I went; when I wanted to learn how to fly a plane, I took the class; when I wanted to write my first book, I did; when I wanted to sell alcoholic freeze pops, I did; when I wanted to create a daily fantasy sports company, I did; and when I wanted to buy a company, I did. Some of these things kicked my ass, some didn't. The ones that didn't were amazing.

CAN'T DO IT ALL YOURSELF

Even though many times it feels like you are the only one building your business, you need help. You need help from vendors, customers, and employees. Without others you will not be able to grow your business. A true entrepreneur has a tough time understanding this. We are control freaks and want to manage everything. I learned a long time ago that this method will not only stunt growth but could destroy you and your business. Asking for help is even harder. But if you don't ask, you will not make it. If you are in a tough spot in your business, you must ask others not only for help, but for their thoughts. As I mentioned earlier, talking through something even when you're in a bind may give others an idea on how to solve the challenge. I can't tell you how many times I have gotten ideas just from talking with my executives, a business partner, or a colleague about a challenge.

TALK WITH YOUR FRIENDS

For a type A personality like myself, someone who never wants to look weak, asking for help can be gut-wrenching. There are ways to ask without asking. For instance, talking about your business and asking how others would handle a situation may spark an idea you never thought of. So talk with trusted associates or a mentor.

And finally . . .

IT'S NOT A DEAL UNTIL THE CAR DRIVES OFF THE LOT

Business is a very emotional world. When you close a deal or make a sale, there is a sense of pride and joy. Some people want to jump up and down and tell the world about their triumphant sale. The challenge is that too many people prematurely tell others, especially their colleagues, that they closed a big sale. I've seen it time and time again, from a basic $100 sale to a $100 million deal, where one side boasts that they "closed the deal" and breaks open the bottles of champagne. I recently finalized a deal where I will be appearing in a major film with Scarlett Johansson and Kate McKinnon. Now that last sentence could be interpreted many ways. Some may think I will be acting in the movie, some may think there is a quick cameo of me. Several months ago I was presented with the opportunity to license my advertisements in the movie, which is called "Rough Night." I must say I was immediately excited and wanted to tell the world. I will admit I told a few close friends about the possibility but it was far from a done deal. Last week we signed the agreement and as far as I can tell I will be in several scenes in the movie. Now, at the time of the printing of this book, it may be possible that the scenes in which I was to appear were left on the cutting room floor. But for all intents and purposes, the deal is done.

I've had executives come to me with a huge smile on their face, all pumped up to tell me how they closed a huge deal. I would ask questions like, well is the contract signed, and they would say no, but it will be. Okay, have we received any money? No, but it's coming, they would say. The days would come and go, and no contract was signed and no money was received. The executives now looked silly and their credibility was shot. Don't tell people, especially your colleagues, that a deal is done until the ink has dried and money has exchanged hands.

When I was selling cars we had many deals fall apart. We called those deals flakes. You would go through the whole selling process, from test-driving, to negotiating price, to even signing the contract. Then the customer would "flake." They wouldn't answer their phone, and never came in to pick up the car. So, what a salesperson thought as a done deal wasn't in fact a deal. Now, legally, were we good to go? Yes, but from a business goodwill perspective, we just let it go most of the time. So, even though you have worked hard in your business and closing deals, don't count those deals or even tell others until everything is totally wrapped up. Understanding that deals may fall apart and mentally preparing for what could happen is a great way to prepare and think about potentially restructuring the original deal, or trying to salvage what you thought was an actual deal.

CHAPTER 10

Making Money Doing Nothing

"Anybody who tells you money is the root of all evil doesn't fucking have any."

—BEN AFFLECK, "The Boiler Room"

In this section we are going to be discussing making money and about some of the mistakes people make. We'll talk about what's realistic, what's really going on out there in the business world, and how to increase your income. There is no get-rich-quick scheme out there. There is no magic bullet, no magic pill that you're going to be able to take like in that movie "Limitless"—although some would say our brain formula Clarizene by Cloixonné is pretty close.

There are plenty of guys out there offering self-help, life coaching, or business development who say, "I'm going to show you how to go from zero to seven figures." Most people aren't even paying attention to what that means. That's from zero to a million dollars. You may have seen these guys on Facebook, Instagram, Snapchat, Twitter, or YouTube saying they're going to show you how to go from zero to a million dollars literally starting from nothing.

It is the most unrealistic whacked-out fraud I've ever heard of. What they're really doing is they're selling you some out-of-the-box kit on how to make money. What they're not showing you is something realistic. And most of it is not tangible stuff. It's just vapor.

In your job and in your personal life, what can you do at this very moment to make more money? Because that's what most people are talking about, right? Most people aren't looking to get a new job right away, and they're not looking to dive into uncharted waters. People are working day in and day out, and they're looking for ways to increase their net worth. That's the realistic thing about what we talk about here at Blue Vase and Cloixonné, and the things that we're discussing throughout this book. We're talking about increasing your net worth and actually making more money.

You are not going to make a million dollars tomorrow, not next week, and not next month. Not going to happen. If that's what you're looking for, put this book down and read another book, because that's not what I'm going to tell you. It's not realistic.

I saw this guy on Instagram today who says, "I'm looking for motivated people. Only motivated people that are looking to make six figures. Is there anybody right now that would like to make an additional six figures?" Of course. Everybody would! It was the most ridiculous call to action I have ever seen. You know what it was? It was just another one of these network marketing companies with a generic pitch selling people an unrealistic dream.

I was general counsel of a network marketing company years ago, long before we launched Cloixonné. I saw real money being made by real people. Real money, millions of dollars, exchanged hands in this network marketing company, and it's happening now at a much faster scale and bigger level with Cloixonné. But there is no secret on how to make money in network marketing. It doesn't just happen overnight. The people in these network marketing companies who tell you it can happen quickly are the exact people we kick out or preclude from joining Cloixonné. There are some great companies and opportunities in this world. The long-term companies that will sustain growth are the ones who are realistic and honest about the opportunity. Before I launched Cloixonné, I had dozens and dozens of people I didn't even know reach out to me from the network marketing world. They all pitched me on "systems" that work and recruiting methods or compensation plans that would "skyrocket" our growth. When you look deep into their souls, these guys were just looking for a way to get in at the beginning and ideally make some money, then get out. I had one guy actually say to me that we could make "good money for a few years." A few years? They couldn't care less about me, my customers, my products, or my employees. This is a key point I want to drive home. You must care about yourself, your customers, your products, and your company for the long term. Nothing good comes of short-term money. Get rich slowly, not quickly. Put in the work, believe in the system, and be consistent, and you will be successful in anything that you do.

Business Building Tip

Get rich slowly, not quickly. Put in the work, believe in the system, and progressively realize your goals every day.

Network marketing companies or these affiliate marketing companies will prey on your excitement by telling you there's quick money to be had. But the people finding real success at direct sales companies and network marketing have been in their roles for a long time. These guys and gals are building something that is sustainable and realistic. They're building on it day in and day out. That's what's really happening.

Imagine you find this joker online who's going to show you how to go from zero to seven figures and you're all excited about it. He says to you, "You have to essentially dive in 100 percent." You have to give 105 percent effort, which isn't even a real number. Give a 105 percent 100 percent of the time. It's not realistic.

Human beings can't sustain that. We can't sustain 105 percent, but what we can sustain, what is possible, are baby steps. The premise behind my last book, *5% More*, is that anybody can do anything 5 percent more or 5 percent better. It's a scientific fact. To acquire long-term sustainable money, one of the fundamental things that absolutely works is doing a little bit more each and every day.

Let's say you're doing nothing right now. You're at the bottom of the bottom, not doing anything. The first step is do something, get started. Let's say you're a mid-level manager, let's say you're a vice president, let's say you're just another number at a company. If you truly want to make more money, have long-term sustainable success, and increase your net worth, you need to do a little bit more than everybody else.

Another key point is that you need to do 5 percent more without thinking you are going to get compensated for it. Now that blows people's minds. They say, hold on a second, I'm a twelve-dollar-an-hour guy (or nine or fifteen dollars, however much), and you're telling me that you want me to do more? Yeah, that's what I'm telling you. You want me to do more and possibly not get paid for it. Sounds crazy, doesn't it? It's not crazy. It works. We're talking about increasing your net worth, we're talking about really making money.

The title of this chapter is "Making Money Doing Nothing." I recently ran into some young people who look at celebrities and someone like Floyd Mayweather, who flaunts his affluence. He flaunts that he made $120 million dollars in one of his last fights. He is the highest-paid professional athlete in the history of sports. Or young people see billionaires out there, such as Bill Gates, Warren Buffet, and Mark Zuckerberg. They see how much money these people are making, and they say, "They're making money doing nothing." Right now, they probably are making money doing nothing, but they didn't "do nothing" to get there.

I make money in my sleep, but it took me a long time to get there. By creating businesses, and intellectual property that is sold all over the world, sales are being made, business is being conducted even when I sleep. But you have to build your foundation like I discussed earlier in the book. You have to put the work in before money can be made in a way that appears to be without effort.

Look at people in the Hollywood music industry. Adam Levine, Taylor Swift, Lady Gaga, Usher, and other famous musicians with hit songs are making tons of money. They're living the life that you and I would dream about, but they didn't get there just by doing nothing. Take a look at Nick Cannon. He was a host on "America's Got Talent." He's a DJ, a standup comedian, a musician, and a spokesman for RadioShack. That guy is probably the hardest-working guy in Hollywood. In fact, a couple of years ago he was hospitalized when his kidneys were going to shut down because he probably wasn't drinking enough water while he was running around. That guy is working his ass off.

Love him or hate him, or any other celebrity out there. They're working very hard. They're not just doing nothing.

How does this apply to you? How can you truly make more money? There are a lot of different things you can do, but it all goes back to what I said earlier and it's real simple. (And again, this stuff works.) Are you going to see money today? Tomorrow? Maybe, you actually might, depending on how you apply what you are learning in this book. I've done the research and I've interviewed people. I've interviewed professional athletes and businesspeople. I've read studies about success, personal development, personal growth, and about wealth. All it really takes is just a little bit more effort, a little bit more than where you are right now. When you get past that first step, we can talk about 5 percent compounded. Five percent compounded means doing more than what you did the day before and it's compounding. It's growing like interest.

Too often people wait for something to happen because they feel as though they are entitled to success. What do they do all day? Nothing, and no money is ever made doing nothing. Go back and read this section again. I know some of you may feel as though this is some sort of incoherent rant about other marketers that aren't me. I want you to really think about what I'm saying.

TRY THIS: IT WILL HELP YOU UNDERSTAND

If you're a salesperson, let's say you set a goal of a hundred phone calls a day. You meet that every single day, and every week your paycheck pretty much stays the same. You're comfortable with that; you're doing okay. You pay your bills, but you're still living week to week. Next week, make 105 phone calls per day. See what happens. It's that simple, but it works. This applies to every aspect of your life. Whatever you're doing, whatever your goal is, do 5 percent more next week. Now you may be saying, he is just trying to sell me *5% More*. I'm not, in fact the 5% number is a bit arbitrary. Just do a little more each day and the making money starts to happen.

LET'S TALK A LITTLE MARKETING

What is the best way to market anything? Well, if you ask one hundred people this question you may get one hundred different responses. Some will talk about social media, some will talk about building brand awareness, some will talk about customer acquisition, some will talk about human psychology and what makes people buy, and so on. I have spent over $100 million marketing and advertising products across multiple industries, from the liquor business to the book business, to NASCAR, to retail, and of course direct marketing. I have managed campaigns that I own and I've also managed campaigns for others that have generated over $1 billion collectively in revenue. Direct marketing in my humble opinion, is the only way to market anything. Direct marketing is a type of marketing where you directly market to the consumer in an effort to get them to act on something. *Usually, it is to buy a product or a service.* The last line is the key to growth and success in marketing. For any dollar you spend, you must be able to attribute some sales to that very dollar. Do not ever spend a dollar in marketing without knowing what your return on investment will be. It doesn't have to be a one-to-one or two-to-one ratio. It could be less than one-to-one. But, you must make something for every dollar spent. How can you spot direct marketing these days? Simple, any advertisement with a web address, telephone number, text prompt, short code, or QR code within the advertisement is a direct marketing campaign. Even the large major brands that have money to spend on building their brand awareness without making a dollar on that very advertising are now putting these things into their advertisements. I could and very well may write an entire book on marketing, but this is a valuable lesson. I have "brand experts" always trying to get my business, even for this very book. My first question is, if I spend X amount of dollars with you, how much revenue am I going to bring in. Ninety-nine percent of these so-called experts, can't and won't commit to a number. Spending money on an ad, an e-mail campaign, a direct mail campaign, or a television campaign is easy. Generating revenue from that very ad is the key to marketing success.

Business Building Tip

Do not ever spend a dollar in marketing without knowing what your return on investment will be.

LET'S TALK LOCAL

Here is a quick example that happens all over the country with small local businesses. Let's say you own a coffee shop that serves breakfast, bagels, donuts and (obviously) coffee. Now let's say one of the local publications, one that is distributed in the town you are in and maybe a couple other surrounding towns, asks you to take out an ad that will run a couple of weekends. Let's say that ad is only $200. Many small businesses make the mistake of sending in maybe a picture of the owners in front of the business with their hours of operation listed and maybe their website. Sometimes they may have a nice picture of the inside of the establishment with the same information on it. Most of the time the business will rely on the publication to create the ad for them. The publication just wants your money. They aren't marketers. If you are in business, then you have to be a marketer. The smart thing to do for this ad would be to create a coupon that potential customers would bring into the business. Something aggressive, like HALF OFF breakfast and a FREE cup of coffee with about a monthlong expiration date. What this will do is generate revenue and attract new customers. I know you may be saying to yourself right now, this is basic stuff. Well, it is and it's expandable to virtually all types of businesses. That coupon is a call to action that will most certainly get people through the door.

Now, if not one person comes through the door, there is a problem. It is either the ad, or the placement of the ad in the publication, or the distribution, or all three. By putting a coupon in, you can track how well the ad performs, and you can go back to the publication and ask them again to run for FREE. Most publications will. Why? Well, they want your continued business, and they don't want you telling others that their publication doesn't work for local businesses which essentially pay for their publication. If you just put an ad with your pretty face on it, you will never know if that $200 was worth spending.

There are all sorts of creative things you can do with your marketing that will engage your customers and generate revenue.

You know your business better than anyone. You may not be a professional marketer, but you can think of things that will help make you money. This basic example rings true and works in the current digital age we live in and with any business. Following are three marketing tips:

1. If you are in business, you have to be a marketer.
2. Marketing dollars *must* bring in revenue.
3. Create a call to action to get the customer to buy.

STORIES SELL, NOT PRODUCTS

What really sells something, whether it be a service or a physical product is the story. Right away, some of you would say, "Well that's not true. The product sells itself most of the time." Not true. If you want to create a company and sell a ton of product you need more than just a product. You need a story. There are thousands of products out in the marketplace that never see the light of day because they don't know how to tell stories. There are a million other books out there that are probably better than mine, but I know how to tell a story and be entertaining. We will talk entertaining later.

When you are building your business, which for many of you is your brand. Meaning YOU. In other words your brand is the business. You are selling the story of YOU. Look at Instagram and Facebook and Snapchat and Twitter. What you click and scroll through are "story lines" The huge stars out there are selling you on their story. Kim Kardashian is selling the story of her day-to-day life. Her reality show is selling her product, which is ultimately her telling you the story of her life. Look at some of the great ad campaigns out there now. They are either entertaining you, telling you a story, or doing both. The product is almost secondary.

LET'S BUY A LITTLE INSURANCE

GEICO, for example, is an insurance company that most of you know. I'm not saying GEICO is the best or even that it has the most revenue, but it's their marketing I am talking about. Now, in most states the insurance industry is regulated and a company like GEICO has to offer the same type of policies with the same pricing structure as all the other companies. It has changed over the years but that's still valid for the most part. So, in order for a company to compete, they need a way to market. You know who GEICO is because of their entertaining story about the cute little gecko and his life. They created a story around a gecko and it's entertaining, and now you have their insurance. Why? Is GEICO really better than all the rest? Or is it pretty equal? Sure there probably are some differences, but for the most part it's pretty similar to other insurance companies offering the same coverage.

What about Progressive? You know Flo? I bet you do. We know her so much that people dress up as her during Halloween and you know exactly who they are dressed up as . . . Flo. How about another insurance company? How about Farmers? You know them too. They focus more on the storytelling than the entertainment. They tell you crazy stories of claims that they covered and they make those stories entertaining. The product, which is insurance on your home or car, is almost secondary; what's important is how they sell the story and entertain you. Create a fun and entertaining story and you'll have a winner.

JOINT PAIN

Joint pain is a problem for people all over the world. There are all sorts of solutions both pharmaceutical and natural. My company focuses on the natural ways to help people with many ailments including joint pain. When you go to GNC there are over forty joint health solutions. Some labels are very basic, while others are fancy. Some have more retail space than others. Some are better than others. When you scour the Internet you find the same thing. But, the most successful ones tell a story. They tell a compelling story that people are actually entertained by, meaning they are interested in the message and maybe it resonates with them. Back in 2009, when I decided to host my own infomercials we knew of a guy name Jim Shriner. He is a dynamic character, as genuine as you can get, and he has a great story. A story about how pain affected him and his family, including his wife. I also knew that he had been taking a product for a while that helped him. I asked him if he was willing to tell his story to me in an effort to help others and build a business. At the time I did not have much experience in front of the camera. I did not have a studio, nor the resources to rent a studio in Hollywood. But I knew Jim had a story that was entertaining and would sell.

I found a company in Gloucester, Massachusetts, that claimed to have a studio. We went there to check it out. "Studio" was a very generous way to describe this place. It was literally in the basement of a house built in the eighteenth century. There was no proper lighting, there was no proper backdrop, I didn't have wardrobe or makeup. But we had cameras and a place to film, a basement in a sleepy fishing town. Well, we shot that infomercial and it's still on air to date, and we have sold over $100 million worth of that product. It built my company and has helped hundreds of thousands of people. Now here is the secret. The product does in fact have what we call in marketing a "unique selling proposition." The ingredients we use are not very common, although not super rare. But it was the story that sold the product, not the product selling itself. Here is another secret. The production value is horrible. I'm orange, he's pale, you can see the black backdrop when you are not supposed to, we have what are called "jump cuts," which means we make a hard cut that looks weird. All of this happened because we didn't really know what we were doing and we were broke. But the production value doesn't matter. It's the story. So when you are creating your story, don't get bogged down in the production quality, although in this day and age with what our phones and apps can do, you can create kick-ass content that looks like it was shot in Hollywood. Remember the story first.

PEOPLE, PRODUCT, PROCESS

I'm a fan of the show *The Profit* on CNBC featuring investor and business person Marcus Lemonis. He has said over and over again that what makes businesses successful are three core principles: the people, the product, and the process. If you see the dedication to my book you will see that I agree 100 percent about the people. Without good people your business will not thrive and grow. You need good people. Earlier I mentioned trusting the process throughout. Without a process or a system you will be lost. But here I want to touch on the product. You can have a great story that creates sales and generates customers, BUT if you don't have a great product supported by a great process as well you will be out of business. Very early on I touched on the importance of a great product. Whatever it is you are selling must be great. You can have the best story in the world, but if you can't deliver the goods from the story that you told, you will not make it. Now does this mean your product has to be perfect before you enter the market? In most businesses it does not have to be perfect. But you need to do your best to get close to perfect before you launch. If you think your product is great, adds value, and works, but could be improved upon later, that's okay. You can still sell it. People aren't looking for perfection, they are looking for something that helps them solve a problem or makes their lives better. Chase perfection, but don't worry about getting there, because you most likely will never achieve perfection.

THE CUSTOMER

There are great resources out there that can help you with your front-end process. In today's world that usually means your website. Russell Brunson created what he calls "Click Funnels," which are out-of-the-box websites that he admittedly ripped off from others. He's not necessarily using the content, but many times some of the content and the look and feel of a website for a particular industry. I don't know Russell, but I watched a bunch of his videos and he seems like a good guy and a very solid marketer. Remember what I said earlier, success can be duplicated. That's really all he is doing, and it's really all I have done. There are tons of other resources that can help you build cool websites with all the bells and whistles even if you lack coding skills. It's pretty wild what you can get now. But the front-end process is easy. Selling to someone is easy. Maintaining them as a customer and providing great customer service are other key elements to success in business. I started out in the direct response business working in a call center in a tiny cube in the customer service department. I watched firsthand what NOT to do. You must be able to support the process by providing great customer service. Here are a few tips:

1. If you sold to someone early in the morning, you should be able to provide customer service at the same time or close to it.
2. Respond as quickly as you can to all customer inquiries.
3. Get ahead of a challenge, which means that if there is a problem with a customer order or product, let the customer know.
4. Maintain a rapport with the customer on an individual level.
5. Don't always try to sell them something. Offer them free valuable things and they will be appreciative.
6. Treat the customer how you or your mom would want to be treated.

7. Take customer service calls or inquires and do it yourself. What you will learn will help improve your level of service. Remember Rich the accountant?

If you follow these basic rules, then the next chapter will be easy for you to understand and implement in your business life.

CHAPTER 11

Stop Caring

People actually care too much about things, plain and simple. Caring too much actually inhibits their ability to grow. What do I mean by that? It's such a crazy thing to say. Mike, are you saying that I shouldn't care about my job, my business, my life, my children, or my work ethic? No, no, that's not what I'm saying.

One of the things that I think is happening today is people care too much about what other people think and say. What exactly does that mean? Now, I care about my reputation and that is different from caring what people think and say. I'm sure you care about your reputation if you're reading this. Most likely people care about their reputation, but the challenge is that too many people care about what other people think and say.

The day I stopped caring about what other people think is truly the day when I was set free. It may sound a little weird, but it's a reality. The day I stopped caring is the day I actually started to grow. I remember where I was and I remember whom I was talking to. There was a real moment in my life when I just said, "I am no longer going to care what other people think about me." It's a really, really hard thing to do, because it's hard to separate things like your reputation which is something you care about from what people say and think. People care about their reputation, and I will explain the difference in a bit about your reputation and what people think or say.

If you're a righteous person doing the right thing, running a good business, and helping people, and if you get up every day to be a good, productive citizen, then what others think and say doesn't matter. By the way, there are a lot of bad people on this planet. Those people *should* also care about their reputation, because they are the ones who are really setting society back. Those are the ones who are looking at you on Facebook and trying to bring you down. Those are the ones who are taking shots at your life. They are the types of people that we definitely shouldn't care about.

REALITY

When we're on Facebook, Twitter, or Instagram, we are so worried about what other people perceive our lives to be like. On social media, too many people are lying to themselves and projecting an image to the whole world—an image that's not a reality.

They do that because they care what other people think about them. If you spent more time actually focusing on your life and working toward a goal that truly reflects what you're portraying to the rest of the world, then it becomes a lot easier to care less about what other people think. You see, when I stopped caring about what other people thought about me, I truly was set free. I said to myself, "I am no longer going to worry about what other people think, and how they perceive me." I know who I am and what I'm doing.

Now, as I said earlier, I do care about my reputation, but I don't care about some jerk who feels that I'm somebody that I'm not, and I don't care about people who see me as an infomercial guy. Maybe they don't like what I do or they don't like the products that I sell, and that's okay with me—they don't have to. It was very, very difficult to come to terms with this, because everybody wants to be liked, including me. Everybody wants to be perceived a certain way, including me.

But when we spend so much mental energy thinking about how other people perceive us, it becomes an emotional drain on us and brings us down. However, if you live your life the way you really want to, and in a way that is like the images you're projecting onto social media outlets, then you won't care what other people think—because you know who you are. It's very, very difficult to do, and sometimes even I forget, but stop caring about what other people think and you will be set free in your business and personal life.

CARING IN BUSINESS

In this day and age where everything is reviewable on sites like Yelp, Google, and Amazon, your reputation is very important and you should care about it. However, you will have people who give you bad reviews or post negative things. Some people will just be nasty. If you are the person I described earlier, with a business doing the right thing, putting out a great product, and providing great customer service and support, then you shouldn't care about the one or two bad reviews. I own several businesses and sell dozens of products. We get reviews all the time, and sometimes they are blatantly not true. The good ones outweigh the bad ones though, if you are running a solid business that cares about its reputation. This book and my earlier books will get bad reviews. Fuck them. I know the content provided in my books provides value and helps people. That's all I need to care about.

I have a friend who owns a small restaurant. She is constantly responding to reviews that are under five stars. My first response to her was, why are there so many bad reviews? She looked perplexed. I asked her if she cared about her reputation. Of course, she said yes, that was why she was trying to defend her bad reviews. I explained to her that it was too late and she was really caring about what other people think and say. Once those reviews are up, it doesn't matter, the damage has been done. If you consistently provide a good service and experience, then defending bad reviews will be a thing of the past and everything else will fall into place.

Here is a little caveat about not caring, especially in this reviewable world we live in. If you sell a product or provide a service, it is not a bad thing to look at your bad your reviews once in a while, solely for the purposes of objectively listening and then making changes if the review was accurate. I told my friend to look at her restaurant and the quality of the service and food and see if there can be improvement. She did, then made some improvements and does not worry about the bad reviews. Her business is now booming. Why? She stopped caring and focused on what really matters.

Business Building Tip

Care, just not that much.

NEVER SECOND-GUESS YOURSELF

I'm concerned about my reputation, but I don't really care what other people think about me or what I do in my life. The moment when I stopped caring about how others think about me or my decisions happened early on in my career at Blue Vase. I was still essentially practicing law for myself, which they say you should never do. I second-guessed a decision that I had made from a legal perspective, and I was right. That day, even though I was right, I told myself that I was no longer going to second-guess myself, because we can get overwhelmed and burdened by the thought process of saying, "Did I make the right decision? Am I doing the right thing?" I second-guessed myself because I cared what other people thought if I was wrong. We are wrong all the time. Worrying about how others perceived my decision-making ability interfered not only with my business but with my own personal psyche.

If you truly are a righteous person who is trying to do the right thing and put forth your best effort, but you were wrong, that's okay. That's really okay. That day I happened to be right, and it really bothered me that I second-guessed myself. I second-guessed myself based on opinions of other people who, quite frankly, were smarter than me. They had a much better pedigree in terms of educational background, but this particular decision I made had an impact on my business. If you are the CEO, no one knows your business better than you. Especially if you are the type of CEO who does the things that need to be done in order to succeed. I know my business better than anyone. Education has nothing to do with making good decisions. Intelligence has nothing to do with how to be successful in life.

Before I stopped caring about what other people think and stopped second-guessing myself, my life was really in turmoil. I was broke and had tons of personal debt. I was essentially living a life that was unhappy. As soon as I stopped caring about how others perceived me, my life started to get better. Did it immediately change, in that all of a sudden I became this super wealthy, super happy, perfect person? Absolutely not, but this step allowed me to move forward, and will allow you to move forward and prosper as well.

Another pivotal moment in my business and personal life was when I stopped caring about what other people thought of me on Facebook. A friend of mine said to me, "Hey, did you see what so-and-so said about you on Facebook?" By the way, this so-and-so happened to be somebody who I fired because of incompetence. My friend said that this post was public and everybody could see it. I said, "No, I don't really care who it is, what they're saying or to whom they're saying it. I don't care who's spreading it, forwarding it, or e-mailing it. I don't really care." She couldn't believe it.

She said, "Mike, it's really, really nasty stuff." I didn't care, because I know who I am. I know what I'm doing with my life. I know when I make mistakes or screw things up. But I also know where I'm going, or at least where I'm trying to go. I see so many people on Facebook, Instagram, and all these other social media outlets perpetrating a fraudulent image. I'm someone who's out there on all of these social media networks, but the things I post and the things that I say are truly my life. I'm not posting pictures of a perfect life and a perfect lifestyle and all these other things that aren't a reality.

To some people my lifestyle may be much better than theirs, and quite frankly it probably is, but that's not the point. I really don't care what other people think about what I'm doing. If someone doesn't like what you're doing, you have to stop caring. Once you're able to redirect that mental energy to focus on the true endgame—moving forward and getting better in life, getting the things you want in life, and achieving your goals—you're able to remove negative energy from your brain and stop caring about what other people think.

This idea is really simple to understand, but for some it's very, very difficult to implement. I'll be honest with you about that person who said something really nasty about me. I said I didn't want to know about it and I didn't want to see it, but I went back weeks later and found the post. You know what, it hurt. I said, "That's not me, why would he say that? That person is just a disgruntled employee and quite frankly not anybody that I even care about." He's just a bad person. He did drugs, spent most of his time going to concerts, and didn't care about his own kids. I fired him because he was negative and incompetent. These people, by the way, are the ones in society who are trying to bring others down. Due to their incompetence and insecurities, they try to make themselves feel better by attacking others. When you think about that, it's easy not to care. Why would you care about some loser attacking you? You shouldn't.

I MAKE CANDY—I'M NOT A FRAUD

Napoleon Hill in *The Law of Success* talks about this subject as well. He tells a story about how when he was younger he owned a confectionery, a candy factory, with two other people. These two other people essentially kicked him out of his own company because of greed. They didn't want to split things in thirds. They trumped up charges, and they made him look like a criminal.

He talks about what he could have done. He could have gone after them and sued them, and could have really made a big stink. But he decided he wasn't going to do that. Rather, he was going to move forward because he knew who he was. Reading that story, I thought about how I had done the same thing a couple years prior. That was what really solidified my decision to stop caring about what other people think.

When you go to bed at night, shut off your computer, and stop tweeting, texting, and posting on Facebook, your reality is right there. Your reality is who you really are on the inside. You can't get away from that. You can't hide from that. When you lie to yourself, it just gets worse. Sometimes you lie to yourself so much that you feel as though the lies are your reality, but they're not. There are so many people who lie to themselves. They project an image to everybody else to show they are living this wonderful life, but they're really not.

You should stop doing these things today. Stop projecting as if you're somebody else, and stop caring about what other people think. When you stop caring what others think, one of the things that will happen is that you'll stop posting a lot. You're going to post a lot less on Facebook, Twitter, Instagram, and all the other platforms. Now, I do post on Facebook and Twitter. I have a different business and lifestyle from most of you. Many times, I post in an effort to motivate people, to help people.

You know what? Some people don't like it. Some people think I'm pompous or arrogant, or whatever they think. But the best part about it is that I don't care what they think. If you don't like it, don't respond and don't talk about it, just unfollow or unfriend me. Sometimes I see people on Facebook saying, "You know what, I unfriended all these people who weren't truly my friends." Ninety-nine percent of the people on Facebook have friends who are not really their friends. It's not really a true social network. They say if you can count five friends on your hand, you're doing pretty well. It's hard to step back to do that sometimes.

I don't want people to misconstrue my point. I'm not saying you shouldn't care about your life, your job, or other people—just stop caring about what those people think of you. The other idea, which I just touched upon briefly, is to stop caring about other people's lives. Focus on your own life first. Focus on where you are and where you want to go. So many of us lose focus by being envious and jealous of other people's lives. I get caught up in that too—everyone does.

FOCUS ON YOU

Now there's nothing wrong with looking at other people and seeing where they are in life and wanting to be there too. But don't care about it so much that it becomes a negative thing in your brain. You're jealous about what they're doing, or what they're saying, or where they're going. You're jealous about your friends' new car, or where they're vacationing, or their perfect kids. You're starting to say to yourself, "Man, that guy is an asshole," and maybe he is. You know what, sometimes I am too and I'm okay with that.

Stop worrying about what other people are doing and focus on what you're doing. Once you start to do that, you start to realize that the only person who has a real impact on where you're going in your life is you. People's Facebook lives are not reality. Everybody knows it. Look, I've been just as guilty as others. Maybe you're posting things because you want everybody to think your life is great, and you want them to see your new car and all these other things, but it's not reality. Maybe you did get a new car, but guess what, now you're paying eight hundred bucks a month for a new Mercedes that you can't afford and shouldn't be driving, because you're living in your parents' basement.

But you got this nice Mercedes so you want to project this image that you're this very successful person. Now that person I just described, a lot of people they care about him and they say, "Man, how does this guy do that?" The person that I just described who got the Mercedes did that because he cares about what other people think about him, when he should really be focusing on where he should be going and not getting that Mercedes that he should have never gotten anyway. But the only reason he got it is because he cares about what other people think about him. It's just a fact. It's a reality. It happens every day but no one wants to talk about it, no one wants to think about it, no one wants to act like they're that person, but a lot of us are.

FOCUS ON YOUR WORLD

We care too much about what other people are doing and what other people think about us. If you live your life in the way you truly believe you should, then nothing else matters, because your reputation will be what you want it to be. You noticed I said I was concerned about my reputation, but I don't worry about my repu-tation. We're all worriers; everybody worries. In this day and age, what is going on in society is very, very scary. Everybody's worried about shootings, the environment, these pseudo-religious organi-zations, and all these crazy things that are going in society.

We're all worried about everything. But I tell people to try to worry less and try to focus on the things that you truly can control. Focus on your life. If you're worried about something in particular, why don't you try and do something about it, rather than worrying? Because it feels a lot better mentally to try to actually do something than worry about it. I tell people that most of time, rather than worry about something, I prepare for it. I prepare for the future and what may happen, but I don't worry about it.

Many of us can become paralyzed by worrying. It's just a made-up thing, and a lot of it has to do with us watching the news. I can't stand watching the news. One of the things that made me want to talk about this is that after watching the news lately, I noticed that I started getting worried myself. But there's nothing I can do, necessarily, other than focus on my life. If there are certain things out there that I want to change, then I need to go out there and do that. Right now I'm focusing on my life, my family, my business, and what I can do to secure my future. That's what I'm "worried" about—but not really, though, right? I'm not worried about it; I'm preparing for it.

I'm preparing for it. It's very, very difficult not to worry, but stop caring about what other people think. Stop caring about other people's lives. Again, what I mean by that is not, "Hey don't care about whether your parents need help, or any of that stuff." The idea is to stop caring about what other people are doing, to stop being nosy. Who cares? And then, stop worrying. These are not the easiest things to do. The first two are, quite frankly, the easiest. Now, the reason why the first one may not be easy for you is because maybe you're not living the life that you know you should be living. Maybe you're doing the wrong things, maybe you're doing drugs, maybe you're out there living a life of crime, or whatever you're doing.

It's going to be a little bit more difficult for you not to care what other people think. But if you're a bad person and you really don't care what people think, then you're probably a sociopath, and I'm not talking about that. I'm talking about real, productive citizens. Quite frankly, I don't think any sociopaths are reading this, and it's too bad for them. Stop worrying about what other people think.

Stop worrying about other people's lives. Then just stop worrying altogether.

Do me a favor, try it for a week. Just try it and see what happens. See if you get more done in a day. See if you're happier. At the end of the day, all we're really talking about is being happy. That's why we're here. It's not about the money, the cars, the houses, the gold watch. It's not about any of that stuff, because if you're not happy then none of that matters. For me, it's always a struggle, so to speak. There are always obstacles and struggles, and there's always going to be heartache.

Life isn't always easy but it doesn't mean you can't be happy. When you stop caring about what other people think and about other people's lives, and you stop worrying about things you can't control—you'll see, it's amazing what happens to your brain. All that negative activity is gone. Now you have all this free space in your brain to do other things, the things that you know you should be doing.

WHAT ABOUT ADVERSARIES?

I've been fortunate to not have many business adversaries. I'm friends with many competitors, and I don't look at the individuals who run the business as enemies. But there are times in business when a direct competitor or a vendor does something that could either hurt your business or get in the way of growth. It could get very contentious at times, so bad that you want to make a call or send an e-mail or text that will blow the whole thing up. I've been there and I've dropped Mother of All Bombs (MOABs) too. But this has to be a last resort. Here is an effective tip when in a difficult situation. Use a third party, usually a trusted executive, as a buffer. Get them involved. They know the objective and the precarious nature of the situation. Use them to essentially save you from yourself. I do it all the time. I'm an emotional human who cares so much about my businesses that sometimes my emotions could blow things up. But if you recall, I also get comfortable with the worst-case scenario before I consider dropping a MOAB. I've dropped a few, but more times than not I was just entering the launch codes—and then the other side sees what I'm doing, capitulates, and we work it out.

CHAPTER 12

Lying to Our Children

It takes time to achieve success. As we've discussed, success means different things to everyone, but no matter what it means to you, you can't get to the top just by hoping for it. It may be a cliché but our children are our future, and your business may someday be passed down to them so it is crucial that they learn, and that you teach them the real life skills now.

We often hear about parents who say, "You can be whatever you want to be, Bobby [or Billy, or Mary]. You can be the president of the United States." It sounds great, and it's awesome to give your kids a goal, but if you don't follow it up with anything, it's never going to happen. You're just going set them up for failure. When you tell your child, "You can be anything you want to be," that is so abstract and open that there really is nothing quantifiable. When you say you can be anything you want to be, it's not a reality. They can't be anything that they want to be. Maybe your child can be a singer a dancer, an architect, or a lawyer, and, yes, maybe even the president of the United States, but it has to be set forth in a manner in which children understand that they're going to experience failure. It's not going to be easy, and there has to be a certain level of realism. We have to tell our kids that there's work to be done to become what they want to be.

I was talking to someone recently who claimed to be an eternal optimist. "I'm an eternal optimist." It's ridiculous. Optimism is great. Having a positive mental attitude is crucial. It's a fact that you control your thoughts; your thoughts don't control you. If you can maintain a positive attitude, that's a great thing. Still, a positive attitude isn't going to get you or your children where they need to be in life. Right now, what's happening all over the country is

143

we're setting up our children for failure. When I'm talking about failure right now, I'm talking about real failure, not just temporary defeats. If you tell your children that they can be the next big thing, without really explaining to them what that means, you're setting them up to be disappointed. If you say, "You can be the president of the United States," and that's all you say, that's what they're going to think, and guess what? They are not going to become president of the United States.

Some people are saying, "Mike, what are you talking about? This is just so crazy. You're being really negative." I'm not being negative. I'm talking about realistic expectations.

In *The Law of Success*, Napoleon Hill talks about the power of one's mental attitude. He lays out a roadmap for someone who really, truly wants to be successful, and he talks about setting realistic goals and expectations. Realistic expectations for what it takes to become what you want needs to be taught to our youth.

ARE YOU HURT OR INJURED?

I started coaching soccer for my daughter's team as an assistant coach. I really don't know anything about how to coach Under 10 (U10) girls' soccer. I'm learning as we go, but it's a lot of fun. One of the things you notice is that they don't keep official score at this level. But guess who is keeping score? The kids are keeping score. There's no way these girls are not keeping score, and that's a good thing.

One of the worst trends now is that everyone's getting a trophy. Everyone's getting a ribbon. That is scary to me. It makes me nervous about what our future is going to look like, because everybody shouldn't get a ribbon; that's just life. If you want that ribbon, if you want that success, stop lying to your kids by telling them that they can be anything that they want to be. You can be whatever you want to be, but say what that is. You can be an architect. You can be the owner of a haunted house. You can be all that stuff, if you actually set forth a series of goals and realistic expectations, and you achieve those goals.

On the field, it may seem like we're teaching our kids soccer skills, but really, at the end of the day, we're teaching life skills: how to win, how to lose, how to work together as a team, how to overcome adversity, how to deal with maybe the differences between an injury and being hurt. My coaches in football used to say, "Are you injured or are you hurt?" because if you're hurt, you can still play. If you're injured, you can't.

In business, are you wounded, or are you down for the count? Meaning have you just lost a sale or a big client, or are you going out of business? If you have resolved yourself to the fact that you are out of business, then you have been fatally injured. What I have found, not only in my own businesses but also in many others, is people think they are injured when in fact they have just been hurt. Business is like the playing field—you get beat a lot, but the game isn't over unless you give up. Throughout the years in my businesses I have had to adapt and modify our processes to survive and grow. We have suffered many wounds and could have succumbed to them, but that's not what I do, what we do, or what any entrepreneur does. You do whatever it takes to stay alive. As the CEO of your company, you know this responsibility falls on you personally. This means that many times you have to personally sacrifice and take risks. If you are able to sacrifice and take some risks, then that means you are still alive in the game. If you can't sacrifice and take the risks when it counts—that is, when you have been wounded and things look dim—then being an entrepreneur isn't for you.

IT'S OKAY TO KEEP SCORE

It's okay to keep score at a certain age. It's okay to talk about winning and losing, because if you don't, we are going to create a nation of spoiled brats who think and feel as though they should automatically get that ribbon or that trophy, even if they didn't even accomplish the goal. Just because they got out of bed and maybe put one foot in front of the other doesn't mean they're entitled to a ribbon. They just got up and acted like a human being. They didn't do anything special, although on a super micro-level it is a successful action. Giving our children a ribbon or a trophy for doing nothing sets them up for failure, and that's a fact.

Winning is important. Losing is important, too. Our kids need to understand how to win and how to lose, and it starts with the parents, coaches, and teachers. We're the only ones who can teach our children these things.

Think about the Butterfly Effect, which is the impact that one person has on one person's life, and then on another person's life. The effect continues to ripple, and the butterflies just keep going and going and going.

As an assistant coach in U10 soccer, the Butterfly Effect really clicked with me, and I thought about the things that we do as volunteer coaches. Our head coach, by the way, is awesome. He's so good. We think not necessarily about winning and losing soccer; rather, we think about the long-term effects of what we're teaching these young children. I take that responsibility to heart—it is very important to me—and I think about what we say to these kids and how we say it. I hope that something we coaches say might be that one moment that these eight-, nine-, ten-year-old little girls remember, something that teaches them some of those life skills that maybe their parents didn't teach them, and helps them get to the next point in life. We coaches are showing them that it's okay to win, it's okay to lose, that they need to work together as a team, that they need to learn how to communicate, that there are consequences to their actions. It's an awesome responsibility, and I love it.

Think about what you're really saying to your children. If they want to be something, then they need to actually do something.

They need to take steps. They need to understand that they can't be successful just because you said they're special. It's a fact.

STOP REACHING FOR THE STARS, UNLESS...

I am a proponent of reaching for the stars, but I say if you want to reach for the stars, then you need to set forth a series of goals. What's your five-year, ten-year, fifteen-year plan? What does your life look like? What do you need to do? The best form of goal setting is to have micro-goals, or daily goals, so that we can have micro-successes.

When my daughter was in second grade, she had to put together essentially an autobiography in the form of a collage. One of the things that her teacher wrote on the bottom was, "In order to be better, you need to do better." Not, "Great job, honey. You're going to be whatever you want to be. You're such a great kid. Congratulations," but positive reinforcement. I'm not saying don't be positive. I am saying that we need to talk about realistic expectations. Let's talk about real life. Real life is hard, business is hard. But when properly setting forth realistic goals, it becomes a lot easier.

Business Building Tip

In order to be better, you need to do better.

I'm not saying I'm the best parent in the world, because I'm not. What I'm saying is you need to give realistic expectations to your children, friends, and family members when they're talking about goals. If you want to be the next CEO, you want to make a million dollars, let's start with the first dollar. How are you going to make the first dollar, and then how are you going to make the next two or four dollars? How is that going to work? What are you going to do? One millions dollars is $2,739.72 a day for a year. How are you going to make that first $2,700.00? Break it down daily so it becomes more realistic AND achievable.

I've said this before, dreams are for sleeping, and it's okay to have an imagination. In fact, in *The Law of Success*, Napoleon Hill talks about imagination. Imagination, by the way, is one of the most powerful things that a human being can harness. Imagination is awesome, and that's okay. We can imagine lots of things, but when I'm talking about real-life goals, real lifetime successes, doing real things, we need to explain to ourselves, and we need to explain to our children and our families, that in order to really get there, you need to set forth goals, and you need to actually do it.

EVERYBODY WANTS TO BE A BEAST UNTIL THEY SEE WHAT BEASTS DO

I'm a big fan of Dr. Eric Thomas and his no-nonsense speeches. One speech I listen to frequently is titled "Beast Mode." You may have seen T-shirts that say "Beast Mode" on them. In this speech he is speaking to a Division 1 football team about what it takes to make it in Division 1. He talks about the work that needs to be done. But what he really drives home is that everybody wants to be a beast until they realize what beasts do. Beasts in business work hard and do the things that most won't do. Beasts in business are doing the work and not worrying about what other people think. Beasts in business aren't posting to the world the work they are putting in. They are just doing it. "When you want it as bad enough as breathing, you will be successful." (taken from https://www.youtube.com/user/etthehiphoppreacher) That's what it takes to be an entrepreneur.

BUSINESS AIN'T SEXY

The fantasy world of being a "rock star" entrepreneur is just that. It's a fantasy, the behind-the-scenes world, the "grind" that so many like to talk about is what creates the sexy images that you see on social media. Sitting down in a boardroom, mapping things out, negotiating with vendors, putting an infrastructure in place—those are the things that really need to be done. In the world we live in today, most of us see the result and that's what we want. We want what Justin Bieber, Taylor Swift, or Usher has, we want what Kim Kardashian and her sisters have. We want what Puff Daddy has and his lifestyle. We want the Ferraris and the houses. But Kim Kardashian, Puff Daddy, Jay-Z, Rihanna, Justin Timberlake, and anyone else you can think of has worked their asses off building their brand. I'm a big fan of the late great actor Eric Lynch. Despite his medical conditions, he worked day and night building his brand. He was on radio and television programs, hosted his own podcast and make appearances in many places. Some of the parts he took were small, but he did them anyway. It took years to build his brand. He didn't just become a household name overnight. And although he didn't reach the same levels of fame and fortune as the previously listed people, if he had lived a full life I'm sure he would have. Make no mistake about it, all of the people listed are all a business. Jay-Z once said, "I'm not a businessman, I'm a business MAN." So, whether it's a celebrity or a person famous on YouTube or Instagram, they are working at it, every day, every night. They are creating systems, they have teams, and they are making decisions daily. I'm not talking about the fake-it-until-you-make-it people. I'm talking about the real ones. So, as you enter this world of business, you have to understand and realize that "The Grind" is a real thing, but success takes more than the grind—it takes everything mentioned in this book.

I don't live your life. I can't tell you what to do, only you know what you need to do. You actually have to do it, and not just believe that you should do it, because people told you that you should do it. If you have made it this far in the book, you obviously want more out of life, you want more for your family, you want more for your business. Only you can make it happen.

In order to continue to grow in that career path, you need to practice. You need to actually go out and do the work. What happens when you do that? You increase what we've talked about before, what we're always going to talk about: your net worth.

I was just talking about overnight successes yesterday with a friend about what I had heard on Howard Stern. Howard had David Spade on the program and he was promoting his new book. David Spade said people often think that someone like himself in Hollywood miraculously is an overnight success. But in reality, for most people who we see out in the public eye, their success was about a ten-year overnight success. Ten years. That's a lot of work, and many people don't want to do the work.

There's no secret to any of this stuff. In order to be better, you need to do better, and that's it. These ideas are really the basic fundamentals of life AND business.

LET'S WRAP WITH UP WITH SOME RED BULL AND EMORY VODKA

Hey now, let's finish up strong and talk about Emory Vodka for a just a little more, because I want to give you this example. I have no illusions that Emory Vodka is going to take over the world in a couple weeks, a couple months, or even a couple years. We have realistic expectations and realistic goals that we've set. One of them is I wanted the vodka to be in four states. We surpassed that goal and we are in six states. Are we knocking it out of the park right now? Absolutely not, because it doesn't happen that way. But we are growing and building brand awareness and brand loyalty.

When you see these "overnight successes," they're not overnight successes. When Red Bull first landed in the United States in the early nineties and essentially created the energy drink market, people thought it came out of nowhere. That's not the case. Red Bull was actually launched in Austria in 1987. It didn't become huge until the 2000s. It didn't just show up out of nowhere. They were doing really well in Europe before even coming to the United States. But they were grinding it out for years before they had their first "overnight success" here in the United States.

At the end of the day, *you* need to go out and do it, and you need to teach your children to do it. Understanding it will not happen overnight, but if you take what you have learned from this book and apply it to your life, things will start to happen for you that will seem like magic. In all reality there is nothing new about success and business. But there are systems, there are lessons to be learned from, there are mentors. It is my hope that you have learned many things from this book so that you too can achieve your goals and live the life you desire. Following the principles in this book will create a blueprint for success and in business. Now go get it!

If you would like some more information about me or my other publications or my podcast The Alden Report, please visit www.michael-alden.com.

You can also find me on
Instagram: @MikeAlden2012
Facebook: @MikeAlden2012
Twitter: @MikeAlden2012
SnapChat: @MikeAlden2012

Finally, if you liked this book, please review it wherever you purchased and share with your friends. Please also post on your social media accounts and tag me along with #BPTB. (In business, you need to ASK!) Bye for now.

More Resources

If you'd like more information about Michael Alden, visit www.michael-alden.com.

You'll find the following resources at your fingertips:

- Michael's Podcast
- How to Subscribe to Michael's Inner Circle
- Michael's Blog
- Related news articles
- Webinar information
- How to book Michael for speaking engagements

WOULD YOU LIKE MICHAEL TO HELP YOUR TEAM REACH THE NEXT LEVEL OF SUCCESS?

Michael Alden is one of America's most popular Direct Response hosts and personalities. His success boils down to his ability to ask more of his clients, his team, and himself. His compelling stories and strategies inspire people across the country to get more out of life and can be used by any person or business. These proven methods helped to build the success of his own company, and he can share them with your team.

If you are interested in having Michael Alden share the techniques that landed his company on *Inc. Magazine's* list of America's fastest growing companies for three years in a row, contact Michael at:

Phone: 978-992-0517

Online: michael-alden.com

E-mail: cs@michael-alden.com

Twitter: @MikeAlden2012

Facebook: Facebook.com/MikeAlden2012

Instagram: @MikeAlden2012

Snapchat: @MikeAlden2012

To purchase bulk copies of *Blueprint to Business: An Entrepreneur's Guide to Taking Action, Committing to the Grind, and Doing the Things That Most People Won't* at a discount for large groups or your organization, please contact your favorite bookseller or Wiley's Special Sales group at special@wiley.com or (800) 762-2974.

OTHER BEST-SELLING BOOKS BY MICHAEL ALDEN

5% More: Making Small Changes to Achieve Extraordinary Results
5% More presents a painless route to change with results that can last a lifetime. Whether you want to boost your health, wealth, or wisdom, this book reveals a key technique that makes it stick. This book shows you how to bring your goals within reach with only **five percent** more effort (**http://fivepercentmore.com/**).

Ask More, Get More: How to Earn More, Save More, and Live More . . . Just by ASKING
Michael's best-selling debut provides an inspirational, pragmatic and simple self-help guide written by a true rags-to-riches everyman and is for anyone looking to improve their lives. In it he outlines strategies and techniques to show how to **Ask More** from yourself and from others to **Get More** from Life.

Peanut Butter and Toast

This illustrated children's book provides a charming story of Morgan and her dad and their mutual love for all things peanut butter. This endearing father/daughter narrative with visually captivating illustrations is the perfect book to share with the young ones in your life (**http://pbandtoast.com/**).

Index

A

Action
the ability to take, 39
direct marketing of your product, 45–46
dumpster diving lesson on taking, 39–40
physical side of taking, 40, 42–43
taking baby steps toward the path of, 42–45
visualization or the mental side of taking, 41–42
Adapting, 66
Alden's Essentials, 65–66
Affleck, Ben, 111
Alden, Michael, 1, 33
The Alden Report (podcast), 21, 45, 57, 61, 151
A.L. Williams (now Primerica Financial Services), 105
Amazon. *See* Social media
Apple, 71
Armstrong, Curtis, 104
Articles of Organization, 27
Ask More, Get More (Alden), 83
Attorneys
business name search by, 26
value of consulting one at the start, 25
See also Legal issues
Avoiding, 100

B

Bar exam failure, 83–84, 86–87
"Beast Mode" speech (Eric Thomas), 148
The Beatles, 63
Beats, 71
Benet, Larry, 99
Bike story, 89–90
Black Panther (movie), 33
Blue Vase Marketing
draftdemons.com venture of, 85
expectations to chip in when necessary at, 74
handling problem with vendor, 102–103
network marketing by, 114
1-800-Flowers lesson learned at, 73–76
plan to build, 55
qualifying script used at, 50–51

relationship capital and connection capital of, 100–101
years of effort into the making of, 21
The Boiler Room (movie), 111
Bottle trademark infringement story, 31–32
#BPTB (In business, you need to ASK!), 151
Brady, Tom, 78–79
Brunson, Russell, 125
Buddha, 41
Buscaglia, Leo, 55
Business adversaries, 139–140
Business basics
intellectual property, 28–33
naming your business, 26–28
patents, 30–31
protecting your business, 25–26
remember that the boring stuff matters, 29–30
value of consulting a lawyer at the start, 25
Business building
being part-time with passion, 16–17
don't jump completely in, 16
don't quit your day job, 20–21
Elf on a Shelf story on raising money for, 17–18
people like to talk and share their knowledge, 15–16, 57
questions to ask for, 21
starting with an idea, 13–14
stop dreaming and wake up for, 18
success can be duplicated tip on, 14–15
ways of finding information, 15–16
Business building tips
about debt, 103
be prepared to adapt when things don't work, 66
for building a sustainable business, 7
care, just not that much, 132
define what success means to you, 62
don't be beholden to organization charts, 74
don't spend a dollar in marketing without knowing return on investment, 119

Business building tips (*continued*)
  focus on the micro-wins that move you forward, 62
  get rich slowly and progressively realize your goals, 115
  to know and not to do is not to know, 57
  never prequalify anyone, or any customers, ever, 47
  nobody wins very time but you need to stay in the game to win, 64
  opportunity comes in the form of new responsibilities, 75
  in order to be better, you need to do better, 147
  people like to talk about their business, 15–16, 57
  questions to help qualify customers, 49
  register several iterations of your website, 34
  success can be duplicated, 14
  value of consulting a lawyer at the start, 25
  verifying inside an organization, 99
  whatever is a worthy goal to you is a worthy goal, 68
  when negotiating, look into the future and anticipate what may happen, 105
  you're never going to be ready, 56
Businesses
  getting started, 13–21
  Marcus Lemonis's three core principles on, 124
  the "secret" to sanity is a sustainable, 7
  undercapitalization as reason for failed, 17
Business ideas
  how to screw up your, 72–73
  it takes capital to launch your, 19
  questions to ask to assess viability of a, 13
  setting up the legalities before proceeding with your, 35
  Steve Jobs' visionary, 13–14
  Zeus Juice started with a, 14
Business names
  creating a separate official entity of your, 26–27
  do a search before selecting, 26
Business plans
  to know and not do is not a, 55
  people like to talk about and share their knowledge and, 15–16, 57
  putting your heart into applying knowing to your, 56–57
Butterfly Effect, 146–147

C
Capital
  needed to launch your business idea, 19
  needed to support a new business, 16–17
  raising the money for getting started, 18
  undercapitalization as reason for business failure, 17
Cardone, Grant, 61
C corp, 27
Chasing after dreams, 18
Children
  the everyone's getting a trophy trend, 144, 146–147
  keeping promises to your, 96–97
  teaching them real life skills, 143–148, 151
  teaching them to be better by doing better, 147–148
  See also Family relationships
Chuck E. Cheese, 39–40
"Click Funnels" websites, 125
CloiXonné
  Alden's Essentials product of, 65–66
  canabidiol (CBD) spray product of, 35
  Clarizene by, 113
  direct marketing system of, 46
  expectations to chip in when necessary at, 74
  network marketing by, 114
  qualifying script used at, 50–51
  relationship capital and connection capital of, 100–101
  success of, 18
  taking action at, 42
Coca-Cola, 28, 31
Communication
  be clear and realistic in the promises you make, 94–96
  dropping the Mother of All Bombs (MOABs), 139, 140
  protecting your relationship capital with good, 101–102
  trust but verify with frequent and honest, 98–99
"Connection Capital," 99–102
  overpromising and underperforming damage to, 93–94
  protecting it with good communication, 94–96, 101–102
  value to success of, 99–102
  what to do when things go south, 103–104
Copyrights, 30
Cruise, Tom, 104

Customers
  direct marketing to, 45–46
  never prequalify, 46–50
  qualifying, 49, 50–51
  realizing that you need your, 107–108
Customer service
  expectations of top-notch, 96
  offer great, 8
  tips on process of providing great, 125–126
Czarface brand, 32, 33

D

Debt
  business tips about, 103
  vendors and, 100, 102–103
Direct marketing process, 45–46, 118–119
draftdemons.com venture, 85
Dre, Dr., 71
Dumpster diving story, 39–40

E

Edelman, Julian, 78
EIN (Employer Identification Number), 27
Elf on a Shelf story, 17–18
Emory, Blake, 64–65
Emory Vodka
  learning from someone's process story on, 76–79
  mistake of prequalifying potential customers, 46–47
  process of marketing, 45
  realistic expectations for slow success of, 150–151
  successes and failures with, 64–65
Emotional Bank Account, 95
Employees
  people as one of the three core business principles, 124
  realizing that you need your, 107–108
  verify by doing what they do, 99
Entrepreneurs
  bike story on doing whatever it takes by, 89–90
  learning that you can't do it all yourself, 107–108
  mentality and drive required of, 35–36
  respect the responsibility of being an, 8
  sacrifice is part of being an, 9
  stop dreaming and just do big things, 18–19
  sustainable business as "secret" to sanity for, 7–8

tips for business that will allow you to sleep better, 8
Zeus Juice example of the daily life of figuring it out, 3–7
Esoteric, 32–33
Eternal optimism, 143–144
Everyone's getting a trophy trend
  as setting children up for failure, 146–147
  the unfortunate, 144–145

F

Facebook. *See* Social media
Failure
  Alden's Essentials as example of success and, 65–66
  bar exam, 83–84, 86–87
  being paralyzed by the fear of, 84–85, 86–87
  be prepared to adapt in case of, 66
  chemical and physical reactions to, 85–86
  the everyone's getting a trophy trend as setting them up for, 144–145, 146–147
  as part of the progressive realization of worthy goal, 66–67
  reconceptualizing it as another opportunity, 88–89
  temporary defeats versus finality of, 83–86
  undercapitalization as reason for business, 17
Family relationships, 96–98
  See also Children
Farley, Chris, 95
Figuring it out, 3–7
5% More (Alden), 88
"Flaky" deals, 109
Freaky Ice (The Netherlands), 14
Future
  always look into the, 8
  prepare for the, 8

G

GEICO Insurance, 122
Get rich quick schemes, 113, 115–116
Gladwell, Malcolm, 63
Goals
  failure as part of the progressive realization of a worthy, 66–67
  get rich slowly and progressively realize your, 115
  Jimmy Iovine's story on using opportunity to reach his, 71–72

Goals (*continued*)
  setting *5% More,* 118
  setting realistic expectations and, 143–144,
    147–148
  success defined as progressive realization of
    a worthy, 61, 62
  teaching children to be better by doing
    better to achieve, 147–148
  whatever is a worthy goal to you is a worthy,
    68
Goldsmith, Marshall, 21
Google. *See* Social media

H
Hard work
  "Beast Mode" speech (Eric Thomas) on
    requirement for, 148
  examples of people making money through,
    116–117
  setting *5% More* goals, 118
  success requires, 63–64, 149–150
  understand that making money takes,
    117–118
Hill, Napoleon, 134, 144, 148
The Howard Stern Show, 71

I
Improvement (constant), 8
Incorporation, 26, 27
Instagram. *See* Social media
Intellectual property
  copyrights, 30, 33
  importance of doing your research, 32
  importance of understanding issues of,
    28–30
  patents and patent infringement, 30–32
  trade secrets and trade design, 31
  as valuable business asset, 30
  website domain registration, 34
  See also Legal issues; Trademark issues
Internal Revenue Service (IRS), 27
Interscope Records, 71
Iovine, Jimmy, 71–72
iTunes, 14

J
Jay-Z, 149
Jobs, Steve, 13–14
Johansson, Scarlett, 108
JUST DO IT!, 106
"Just Do It" speech (Art Williams), 106

K
Kardashian, Kim, 121, 149
Kevin's dad, 50
Kiyosaki, Robert, 8, 33
Knowing/knowledge
  to know and not to do is not, 55–56
  people like to talk about and share their
    business, 15–16, 57
  putting your heart into applying your,
    56–57

L
Law of diminishing returns, 64
The Law of Success (Hill), 134, 144, 148
Legal issues
  don't be a sole proprietor, 26
  naming your business, 26–28
  protecting your business, 25–26
  securing an EIN and proof of
    formation, 27
  setting up LLC (limited liability company),
    26–27
  setting up the legalities before proceeding
    with your idea, 35
  See also Attorneys; Intellectual property;
    Trademark issues
Lemonis, Marcus, 124
Lennon, John, 71
LET's DO IT NOW! story, 106–107
Life skills
  Butterfly Effect of teaching, 146–147
  importance of teaching children real,
    143–144, 151
  taught through teaching kids soccer skills,
    144–147
  teaching children to be better by doing
    better, 147–148
Limited liability company (LLC)
  advantages of a, 26–27
  Articles of Organization, 27
  filing in Delaware, 27
Limitless (movie), 113
Lotto winners, 67–68
Love (Buscaglia), 55
Lynch, Eric, 149

M
Making money
  examples of people who have worked hard
    at, 116–117
  get rich quick schemes for, 113, 115–116

network marketing companies for
  sustainable way of, 114–115
setting 5% *More* goals and start, 118
understanding that it takes hard work,
  63–64, 116–118, 148–150
See also Success
Marketing
  direct, 45–46, 118
  GEICO and Progressive campaigns, 122
  generating revenue from ads as key to
    successful, 118–119
  Jim Shriner's infomercial, 123–124
  learning from someone's process story on,
    76–79
  network, 114–116
  1-800-Flowers type of, 73–75
  by small local businesses, 119–120
  social media buzz, 19, 118
  storytelling approach to, 121–124
  three tips for successful, 121
  See also Products; Services
Marvel Comics, 33
McKinnon, Kate, 108
Mental attitude
  having a positive, 143–144
  for setting realistic goals and expectations,
    144
Mercury Cougar story, 47–49
Mother of All Bombs (MOABs), 139, 140

N
Naming your business, 26–28
National Religious Broadcasters of America,
  106
Negotiating
  a debt situation, 102–103
  "flaky" deals, 109
  if things go south, 103–104
  look into the future and anticipate what may
    happen, 105
  remember that the deal isn't done till its
    done, 108–878
  value of connection capital and relationship
    capital to, 99–102
  when to say "What the fuck," 104–105
Network marketing
  making money through sustainable,
    114–115
  pass on the get rich quick schemes of,
    115–116
Nightingale, Earl, 61, 62, 68
Nike's Just Do It campaign, 106

O
1-800-Flowers story, 73–75
Opportunities
  come in the form of new responsibilities,
    75–76
  how to screw up your, 72–73
  Jimmy Iovine's story on taking advantage of,
    71–72
  of learning from someone's process story,
    76–78
  1-800-Flowers lesson on taking advantage
    of, 73–76
  reconceptualizing failure as another, 88–89
  relationship between responsibility and,
    72–73
  of taking more responsibility on than you
    are paid for, 79–80
  why people fail to take advantage of, 79
Outliers (Gladwell), 63
Overpromising
  how not to engage in, 94–96
  making the mistake of, 93–94
  by parents to their children, 96–97

P
Part-time entrepreneurship
  being passionate and a, 16–17
  lack of capital driving, 17
Passion
  it is possible to be a part-time entrepreneur
    with, 16–17
  putting your knowledge to work using your
    heart and, 56–57
Patent infringement, 31–32
Patents, 30–31
The Patriots, 78–79
Power Players (TV show), 61
Prequalifying
  Kevin's dad story on danger of, 50
  never ever engage in, 46–49
  qualifying versus, 49
Primerica Financial Services, 105
Process
  direct marketing, 45–46, 118–119
  Emory Vodka's marketing, 45
  learning from someone's, 76–79
  as one of three core principles of business,
    124
  tips of providing great customer service,
    125–126
Products
  bottle trademark infringement story, 31–32

Products (*continued*)
  never prequalify potential customers of your, 46–49
  offer one that works, 8
  as one of the three core business principles, 124
  opportunity of learning to sell through, 76–78
  protecting trademark of your, 28–29
  stories are what sell, 121
  two realistic expectations of a, 96
  See also Marketing
The Profit (TV show), 124
Progressive Insurance, 122
Promises/promising
  avoiding behavior when you can't deliver on your, 100
  being clear and realistic when, 94–96
  overpromising and underperforming, 93–94
  trust but verify, 98–99
  in your personal life with your family, 96–98
Proof of formation, 27

Q
Qualifying customers
  prequalifying versus, 49
  script for, 50

R
Reagan, Ronald, 98
Realistic expectations
  for Emory Vodka, 150–151
  stop lying to children and give them, 143–144
  teaching them to be better by doing better, 147–148
Red Bull's "overnight success," 151
Relationship capital
  overpromising and underperforming damage to, 93–94
  protecting it with good communication, 94–96, 101–102
  value to success of, 99–102
  what to do when things go south, 103–104
Relationships
  be clear and realistic in the your promises to others, 94–96
  keeping promises in your family and personal, 96–98
  overpromising and underperforming damage to, 93–94
  talk to trusted, 186

Reputation
  do care about your business online, 131–132
  how other people perceive you versus your, 130–131, 133–134
  you should care about your, 129, 130
  See also Stop caring
Responsibilities
  benefits of taking on more than you get paid for, 79–80
  Butterfly Effect of teaching life skills and, 146–147
  don't be beholden to organization charts on, 74
  1-800-Flowers lesson on chipping in, 73–75
  opportunities come in the form of new, 75–76
  relationship between an opportunity and, 72–73
Rich Dad, Poor Dad (Kiyosaki), 8, 30
Risky Business (movie), 104
Rough Night (movie), 108–109

S
Sacrifice
  as part of being an entrepreneur, 9, 145
  teaching children life skills including how to, 144–145
S corp, 27
Second-guessing yourself, 132–134
Services
  direct marketing of your, 45–46, 118–119
  offer one that works, 8
  two realistic expectations of a, 96
  See also Marketing
Shriner, Jim, 123–124
Social media
  care about your business reputation on, 131–132
  get rich quick schemes found on, 113
  it takes money to create buzz on, 19
  marketing through, 19, 118
  projecting an unreal image through, 130
  stop caring about what people say about you on, 133–137
  story lines and storytelling on, 121
Sole proprietor status, 26
Spade, David, 150
Spouse relationships, 97–98
Stern, Howard, 71, 150

Stop caring
    about what other people think, 129
    about what social media says about your,
        133–137
    focus on you instead of other people,
        136–137
    focus on your world instead of other people,
        137–139
    Napoleon Hill's story on his decision to, 134
    and never second-guess yourself, 132–134
    and spending energy on how you are
        perceived, 130–131
    when there is an adversarial relationship,
        139–140
    See also Reputation
Storytelling
    GEICO and Progressive campaigns based
        on, 122
    Jim Shriner's infomercial, 123–124
    selling through, 121
The Strangest Secret (Nightingale), 41, 61
Stress
    business tips that will reduce your, 8
    as constant in life of entrepreneur, 8
    unique type of entrepreneurial, 36
Success
    Alden's Essentials as example of failure on
        the way to, 65–66
    can be duplicated, 14–15
    defined as progressive realization of a
        worthy goal, 61, 62, 66–67
    define what it means to you, 62
    focus on the micro-wins that move you
        forward, 62
    hard work required for, 63–64, 116–118,
        148–150
    Marcus Lemonis's three core principles for,
        124
    no secret formula but a proven method to,
        68
    Red Bull's slow but eventual "overnight,"
        151
    Russell Brunson's duplication of, 125
    teaching children the life skills needed for,
        143–148
    the 10,000 Hour Rule application to, 63
    value of relationship capital and connection
        capital to, 99–102
    winning the lotto versus becoming a, 67–68
    you need to stay persistent in order to
        achieve, 64–65
    See also Making money

Sustainable business
    as "secret" to entrepreneur sanity, 7–8
    tips for building a, 8
"Sweeper," 71

T
The 10,000 Hour Rule, 63
Thomas, Eric, 148
Tommy Boy (movie), 95
Trade design, 31
Trademark issues
    bottle trademark infringement story on,
        31–32
    Esoteric's Czarface brand, 32–33
    importance of understanding your, 28–30
    naming your business, 26
    website domain registration, 34
    World Wildlife Fund vs. WWE dispute over,
        33
    your own name, 33–34
    See also Intellectual property; Legal issues
Trade secrets, 31
Trust
    trust but verify, 98–99
    when you need help talk to friends you, 108
Twitter. *See* Social media

U
Under 10 (U10) girls' soccer, 144–147
Undercapitalization, 17
Underperforming
    how not to engage in, 94–96
    making the mistake of, 93–94
    by parents to their children, 96–97
United States Patent and Trademark Office
    Website, 33

V
Valuable Final Product (VFP), 93
Vaynerchuk, Gary, 19
Vendor relationships
    business tips about debt and, 103
    connection capital and relationship capital
        in, 99–102
    realizing that you need, 107–108
    what to do when things go south,
        103–104
    when there is an adversarial, 139–140
    when to say "What the fuck," 104–105
    when you owe them money, 100,
        102–103

Visualization
    as mental side of taking action, 41–42
    Steve Jobs's ability of, 13–14

W
Websites
    "Click Funnels," 125
    registering the domain of your, 34
    register several iterations of your, 34
"What the fuck," 104–105
Williams, Art, 105–106
World Wildlife Fund vs. WWE trademark
        dispute, 33
WWW (formerly WWF), 33–34

Y
Yelp. *See* Social media

Z
Zeus Juice
    figuring it out to solve problems of,
        3–7
    keeping day job while starting,
        20–21
    lack of capital problem when
        starting, 17
    started with a business idea, 14
Ziglar, Zig, 42, 64, 83
Zone Diet Company, 5